Technology Made Simple for the Technical Recruiter

A Technical Skills Primer

Obi Ogbanufe

iUniverse, Inc.
New York   Bloomington

Technology Made Simple for the Technical Recruiter
A Technical Skills Primer

iUniverse books may be ordered through booksellers or by contacting:

iUniverse
1663 Liberty Drive
Bloomington, IN 47403
www.iuniverse.com
1-800-Authors (1-800-288-4677)

Because of the dynamic nature of the Internet, any Web addresses or links contained in this book may have changed since publication and may no longer be valid. The views expressed in this work are solely those of the author and do not necessarily reflect the views of the publisher, and the publisher hereby disclaims any responsibility for them.

ISBN: 978-1-4502-1646-3 (pbk)
ISBN: 978-1-4502-1648-7 (cloth)
ISBN: 978-1-4502-1647-0 (ebook)

Library of Congress Control Number: 2010907684

Printed in the United States of America

iUniverse rev. date: 6/30/10

Dedication

For Chris, Chinedu, and Uzo

Contents

SECTION TWO

SECTION THREE

Preface

The technical recruiter is an individual whose job it is to *search for*, *validate*, and *present* qualified candidates to an organization that meet both the technical and nontechnical requirements of the roles they would fill. The understanding of the organization's requirements is the key to searching within the right pool of candidates. The ability to validate the candidate's technical skills to match the organization's requirements varies based on the expertise of the technical recruiter. This book talks about the skills a technical recruiter needs in order to search for, validate, and present the best technical candidates to their hiring organizations.

The typical technical recruiter job description requires a candidate to have a four-year business degree, with good knowledge in Internet search, Microsoft Word, Excel, and Outlook, as well as strong communication skills. Below is an overview of the core requirements found in the majority of technical recruiters' job descriptions.

- Bachelor's degree
- 2+ years recruiting experience
- Excellent communication skills
- Knowledge of MS Word, Excel, Outlook, and the Internet

Notice that there is no required knowledge in technology, networking background, or any business application experience, such as SAP or HRIS. As a result, technical recruiters in recruiting firms or corporate organizations tend to not have technical backgrounds, nor is training in these areas afforded to them.

What You Will Find in This Book

You will discover the essential skills a technical recruiter must develop in the world of technical recruitment. The challenge faced in technical recruiting is this: to understand technology in order to grasp the technical needs of the hiring companies and validate the candidates' skills against the position requirements. Recruiting is a consulting job and, as such, demands that technical recruiters learn and understand the problems faced by their clients.

For example, when filling a software project manager position, a recruiter should know why a project manager with ten years experience and project management certification (PMP) is not suitable for a company that requires a project manager for their software development projects. Could it be that what they really need is a technical project manager? As the recruiting consultant, are you able to ask the kinds of questions that would reveal the real need?

Whether you are new to technical recruiting or an experienced recruiter, this book will guide you in your journey to learn more about the field you are in. You will no longer be intimidated by the technology acronyms in resumes and job descriptions. You will be able to ask pointed and direct questions to understand your client's needs and to validate the technical capabilities of the candidates. You will learn why certifications are required by your hiring manager, what type of system network they have, and which requirements are core to the position.

Who Should Read This Book

Though the primary audience for this book is technical recruiters, this book is for anyone interested in learning the skill sets in the field of technology. A person seeking to change careers and transition into the technology arena will find this book very useful in learning what the requirements are for a specific technical role.

For technical recruiters, whether corporate or contract, new or experienced, this book is an essential technical skills handbook directed at exposing the basics of technology, its foundations, the categorization of skills for certain jobs—such as application development, software testing, software engineering, and enterprise resource planning (ERP)—and the differences between database administration and database engineering and other jobs.

This book will help the technical recruiter talk the talk with candidates and hiring managers with confidence. This confidence will benefit not only the experienced recruiter but also newer recruiters whose desire is to continuously learn the keys of their trade.

The corporate recruiter reading this book will understand more of the technical verbiage and makeup of job roles at his or her current workplace. This understanding will help in creating new job role descriptions that attract desired candidates and also help in implementing first-round interviews to qualify candidates.

Hiring managers looking to complement their current arsenal of technical skills will find this book very useful for interviewing external technical recruiters for the purpose of ensuring the recruiter has the necessary technical knowledge to recruit the right candidates.

Human Resources departments can use this book as a complementary resource guide for selecting internal technical recruiters.

This book is also for individuals who are neither recruiters nor hiring managers but interested in understanding the job roles in technology as a whole.

Where to Start

You can surely jump in anywhere in this book. It is written in such a way that a reader can start from any chapter and flip through to find sample job descriptions and resume highlights of a given job role. There are also sample conversations between the recruiter and candidate sprinkled all throughout this book.

Each chapter ends with a *What We Learned* section, which is a bulleted list of nuggets of information that serve as a reminder of the key concepts of that chapter.

How This Book Is Structured

In this book, you will find thirteen chapters, broken down into four sections. You will find the term client and hiring manager used interchangeably in the course of this book; these terms mean the same. The hiring manager is the client of the recruiter.

Section One (Chapters 1–3)

The *Technical Job Requisition* is introduced in Chapter One as one of the initial documents a technical recruiter encounters. The job requisition is analyzed to find possible questions for the hiring manager. Unless you've recruited the same job description for the same client for several years, you cannot always assume you know what the hiring manager wants in a candidate. Chapter One analyzes a real-world job description to find answers to questions that might have otherwise been assumed or hidden, thus leading to a failed recruiting process.

In Chapter Two we discuss the *Technical Resume*. Though recruiters scan through tons of resumes on a day-to-day basis, it's still important to identify and analyze the selected ones for answers—answers to questions identified from the job requisition. This chapter also looks at the correlation between the resume and job description, how to identify and avoid skill embellishment, and how to ask questions identified from a resume.

Chapter Three looks at the *Technology Team* and the makeup of a technology team. The Organizational Chart is introduced to identify decision makers at the client organizations. This chapter also identifies and reviews the role descriptions of key players in a technology company.

Section Two (Chapters 4–5)

Chapter Four discusses *Fundamentals of Networking* as the foundation for technology as we know it today. In this chapter readers will benefit from information about network layers, types of networks, the advantages of one over the other, and network protocols and how they interact with each other.

Chapter Five deals with *Operating System Fundamentals*. It describes the difference between operating systems, especially the server operating systems versus the desktop operating systems. In this chapter the reader is also introduced to the skills set requirements for major operating systems like UNIX, Windows, and Mainframe.

Section Three (Chapters 6–8)

Chapter Six looks at the *Software Development Life Cycle (SDLC)*, the makeup and process of SDLC and how it affects the development process, and what job descriptions (positions) fit in each phase of the process and how they interact with each other. This chapter also reviews a real-life development process and the part that SDLC plays in it.

Chapter Seven covers *Software Development Technologies* and a description of the types of programming languages. This chapter also reviews how software development is broken up into systems development, embedded systems, and Web application development. Methodologies and frameworks are highlighted here, as well as how to stay current with technology.

Chapter Eight deals with *Software Testing* and how it differs from Quality Assurance, the role of the software tester, and the skills requirements of a tester. This chapter also studies the typical job description of a software tester.

Section Four (Chapters 9–13)

Chapters Nine and Ten discuss the many faces of *Database Technologies* and *Database Job Roles* found in business intelligence, data reporting, database development, administration, data warehouse, and data mining. Chapter Nine also compares two major database software manufacturers and how their software compares to each other.

Chapter Ten describes the major database job roles and analyzes their job descriptions and resumes.

Chapter Eleven addresses *Systems Administration* for Networking and Application Systems. This chapter takes a look at the different networking role descriptions—server administrator, security administrator, the difference between the administrator and engineer roles, and the rise of the "Architect" position in systems administration.

In Chapter Twelve, *SAP ERP Overview*, you will see an overview of SAP Enterprise Resource Planning business applications, the different modules they contain, and their skills requirements.

Chapter Thirteen, *Certification*, answers questions about certification, how it's been devalued over the years, and why companies need certified candidates. Certifications in software development, business process, and operating systems are discussed in detail.

Come walk with me as you learn the technology you talk about every day and, in so doing, gain confidence and become more credible evaluating technical candidates and conversing with hiring managers.

Icons Used in This Book

This book includes notification icons that draw your attention to tips and important and notable information as you read.

CALL NOTES

Call notes are typical questions you can ask the hiring manager or candidates while reviewing job descriptions or resumes.

TIPS

When you see this icon, pay close attention to the information and tips presented in this area.

SAMPLE

This icon shows you sample resumes or job descriptions for the job role in discussion.

QUESTIONS

Pay attention here for special interview questions.

Acknowledgments

My background is in technology, with a bachelor's degree in computer science and engineering. I started my career in NCR Corporation as a professional services consultant and then moved on to other job roles at other companies, including Windows Administrator, Database Administrator, Programmer Analyst, Quality Assurance Engineer, and Database Developer. I am currently working as a Customer Relationship Management (CRM) Consultant and Trainer.

I also worked in the capacity of a technical recruiter in a company I started. During this period, I found myself having to explain on many occasions the differences between one technology and the other; and I began to put together technical questions for candidates and hiring managers. It was during the course of this job that I started thinking about this book. It took the encouragement of other technical recruiters with whom I worked, to whom I would explain the SDLC process, the difference between the Business Analyst's and Project Manager's job roles, or the difference between the SAP functional and technical job roles, to convince me to undertake this endeavor.

Thank you to Christine Udeani and Matt Harrington for their continuous support.

I want to express a special thank-you to my husband Chris, who is the most supportive person I know.

Contacting the Author

If you have any questions regarding this book, need clarification, or simply want to offer your thoughts regarding *Technology Made Simple for the Technical Recruiter*, please feel free to send me an e-mail at obi@indigomark.com. To ensure your email goes to my inbox and not junk mail, please use the following in the subject line: "Thoughts on *Technology Made Simple*."

I will do my very best to respond to you in a timely fashion, but in the case that you do not receive a response in more than one week, please bear with me as I may be unavoidably busy at that time.

Thank you for purchasing this book or just reading a few pages from it as you decide if it will suit your needs. I hope you enjoy reading this book and putting your newfound knowledge to use.

Regards,
Obi Ogbanufe

SECTION ONE

Chapter 1

The Technical Job Requisition

In This Chapter

- Anatomy of a technical job requisition
- Request for information from the hiring manager
- Questions for the candidate based on the job requisition
- The recruiter's take

This book starts with the job requisition because it's the beginning of the process of recruiting. It's the purchase order, job order, or intent to purchase that a client provides to a recruiter that tells the recruiter the profile of candidate to look for. In order to do this successfully, the recruiter needs to really understand what the client wants.

This chapter reviews a typical job requisition, analyzes the demands and skills sets for clarity, and then rates the possibility of finding a candidate that fits the requirement. We will also take a look at the correlation between the job requisition and a resume to see when a resume has been edited to mirror skills from the job description and when a resume truly represents the capabilities of the candidate.

In technical recruiting, as in most professions, the best practice is to stay within a defined expertise. Choose an area of technology to focus on and recruit candidates in this or closely related areas. With focus in a specific area, the technical recruiter is able to dive deeply into an area to learn all there is to know. It also makes it easier for the recruiter to quickly review requisitions and identify (mis)matches. Areas of specialization may be based on specific vendors, such as SAP, CISCO, and Oracle, or may be based on technology implementation phases such as software development, database administration, network administration, and software testing.

There are two reasons why you want to understand the job requisition. One is the ability to assure the hiring manager that you understand their environment and their need and can locate a person for the current position and possibly others. Another reason is the ability to translate this understanding when describing the job role to a potential candidate. Whether you are a contract or corporate recruiter, you must be able to describe the position requirements to a candidate as if you were the hiring manager.

Anatomy of a Technical Job Requisition

When you review a job requisition, you should have a few questions in mind: questions pertaining to the platform, the network environment, the size of company or number of users, the current team if any, the level of expertise sought, any skills mismatch, and the experience of the hiring manager.

Looking at the job requisition in Figure 1.1, Sample SharePoint Consultant job description, a few of these questions have been immediately identified and answered. The level of expertise sought is senior level.

Hiring managers and their human resources representatives know what they want and spend time creating job descriptions that capture their wants and must-haves. Your job as the recruiter is to understand these wants, desires, and must-haves, and be able to separate them to come up with a description that captures realistic demands (based on current talent pool and market forces) and attracts the right kinds of candidates.

When reviewing the job requisition, the first step is to underline or highlight every skills set. You can see these skills sets underlined in Figure 1.1.

SAMPLE

Senior SharePoint Consultant

We have a need for a highly skilled SharePoint Consultant for our office. The primary focus for this position will be solution design, technology leadership, and application development in a SharePoint environment and other Microsoft and .NET technologies. The successful candidate will be responsible for gathering requirements, application design, database design, project team leadership, hard-core development, testing, and implementation.

Engagements range from Enterprise Portal implementations, Extranet implementations, 100% custom application development, to eCommerce, Business Intelligence, Data Warehousing, MS CRM customizations, Enterprise Application Integration, and more. Applicants must have a strong background in a Microsoft development environment including Visual Studio.net, ASP.net, VB.net, C#, MS SQL Server. Applicants must have excellent object oriented development skills, documentation skills, project management expertise, and maintain great professionalism.

Required Minimum Skills:
- Degree in the area of MIS, CIS, or Computer Science
- 5+ years minimum application development experience in a professional environment
- 1+ years of SharePoint experience (MOSS 2007)
- 2+ years of .Net application development
- 3+ years of MS SQL Server
- Database Design skills
- Object Oriented Design skills

Desired Experience
- Experience with Silverlight, Dynamics CRM, BizTalk or Commerce Server
- XML, XSL, ETL, Web Services, and SOA experience also a plus.
- Experience with Unified Modeling Language, Rational Methodology, or MCSD also considered a plus!

Figure 1.1. Sample SharePoint Consultant job description.

The second step is to start identifying answers to the main questions that revolve around the technology environment in the organization—answers that reveal the organization's platform, network environment, existence of legacy systems, number of users, level and type of expertise, and current team.

The platform: During review you must identify the platform, which is usually the main environment in the company. From this requisition we can identify that this company is a Microsoft shop; this means that the company requesting the SharePoint Consultant has a major investment in Microsoft technologies.

How do we know that? It's revealed through the mention of Microsoft technologies all over the job description—.NET, SharePoint, Microsoft SQL Server, BizTalk, Visual Studio, Microsoft CRM, Silverlight, and Microsoft certification. All these point to the fact that this company is heavily invested in Microsoft. So to answer the platform question, you can see that this shop is a Microsoft platform. Because the client is a big Microsoft user, it is possible that the client may also have a partnership with Microsoft. One of the requirements for Microsoft partnership is that a company employ X number of certified individuals. This may account for the desired requirement for the requested candidate to have a Microsoft certification (more on certifications in Chapter Thirteen).

Network environment: Once the platform is identified, the network environment is just an extension of the platform environment. In our example requisition, we identified that the platform is Microsoft; this should point to the fact that this client uses Microsoft network operating systems (more on operating systems in Chapter Five).

Interoperability with legacy: The requisition does not identify any legacy systems in its environment. But you cannot conclude from this that the client does not have a legacy system. It just points to the fact that this is an area that must be clarified with the hiring manager, with a question like, *"Do you have any legacy systems in your environment or any non-Microsoft applications that require interfacing with the current applications?"*

Number of users: Some requisitions give you an indication of how many users are in an environment; our current example does not, and so it needs to be clarified with the hiring manager, with a question like, *"How many* *users are in your SharePoint environment?"* The answer to this question will tell you how many SharePoint users the selected candidate will support. The answer to such a question will also help create a picture you'll use when describing the environment to your potential candidates. Another question you may consider asking to ascertain user growth is "*What is your plan for migrating additional users to SharePoint in the future?"*

Level of expertise: Notice that the requisition is requesting a Senior SharePoint Consultant, but the reference to direct SharePoint experience is "1+ years of SharePoint experience (MOSS 2007)." (MOSS stands for Microsoft Office SharePoint Server.) This may seem like a mismatch, that the client is seeking a senior consultant in SharePoint but requires only about one year experience in the software itself. But reviewing the job requisition further, you will see that the client is looking for a core .NET developer with some experience in SharePoint software. The main development area will be the SharePoint software, hence the title SharePoint Consultant. While the current title may be popular, a more accurate title to engage prospective candidates may be ".NET Developer (SharePoint)."

Type of expertise: This requisition has the title "Senior SharePoint Consultant." The consultant title is usually a confusing one because it can mean different things to different people, so it's wise to clarify the intent from the hiring manager. A consultant can focus on one of three things— development, administration, or project management. This requisition refers to a consultant that is focused on the development phase because of the requirement for development skills and experience in software development tools like Visual Studio.net, ASP.net, VB.net, and C#.

Current team: The requisition alludes to the fact that there are people with different skills sets in this company. Skills sets in this company include Portal implementations, Extranet implementations, custom application development, eCommerce, Business Intelligence, Data Warehousing, MS CRM customizations, and Application Integration. This sounds like a consulting company with engagements with other companies. For some candidates, this is an ideal company where the candidate is exposed to different work environments and industries from month to month, where candidates are never bored. For another candidate, this may be a nightmare because he may prefer a place where he is allowed a learning curve and the ability to learn from teammates, which is not always the case in consulting environments.

Request for Information (RFI)

After careful review of the job requisition, it is time to compile the list of questions and clarifications directed at the hiring manager. The purpose of the request for more information is twofold: to gain clarification on any ambiguity and to confirm your understanding of the needs of the hiring manager. The clarification may include questions not answered from the job requisition, questions that may be asked by potential candidates in regards to the position, and questions to ascertain the most important skills and what makes for the near-perfect candidate.

It may sound as if you are interviewing the client when you start with these questions. In reality, you are. Figure 1.2 illustrates RFI questions for the hiring manager. You want to know as much as possible about the job in order to find the right candidate.

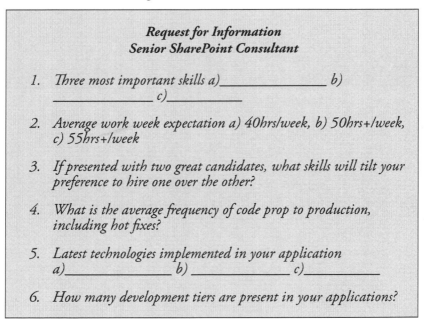

Request for Information
Senior SharePoint Consultant

1. *Three most important skills a)_____ b)*
_____ c)_____

2. *Average work week expectation a) 40hrs/week, b) 50hrs+/week, c) 55hrs+/week*

3. *If presented with two great candidates, what skills will tilt your preference to hire one over the other?*

4. *What is the average frequency of code prop to production, including hot fixes?*

5. *Latest technologies implemented in your application a)_____ b)_____ c)_____*

6. *How many development tiers are present in your applications?*

Figure 1.2. Sample request for more information.

Three most important skills: When reviewing a job requisition, you must identify the three most important skills in the order of importance to the hiring manager. If you are recruiting in an area of focus (e.g., software development), you probably already know the three most important skills, though it still needs to be confirmed with the hiring manager. This will help you identify the required baseline for potential candidates and helps qualify and eliminate candidates quickly.

Average work week expectation: This is an important question to ask the hiring manager. It's important because there are candidates that will not work more than a specified number of hours per week, give or take two hours here and there. There are also employers that require (albeit indirectly) their employees to work an average of fifty hours per week. This may seem irrelevant, but it has caused a number of employees to leave an otherwise great job for another. This also relates to the next question, what the pace of the company is like.

Pace: It's almost a given that a technology or dotcom company is fast paced, though some are more fast paced than others. So it's imperative that you ask the hiring manager the pace of the company.

"What is the average frequency of code prop to production, including hot fixes?"

CALL NOTES

The pace of the company can be identified in this way for a software development or Web-based company. You want to find out the frequency of code propagation in their production environment by asking this question (meaning how many times they move new and updated programming code into their production servers, including hot fixes—which is the software fix of broken code): *"What is the average frequency of code prop to production, including hot fixes?"* The answer will tell you the number of cycles of code a software developer or tester goes through per week. The answer from the hiring manager may range anywhere from "once a week," "twice a week plus one or two hot fixes," "once every two weeks," to "once a month."

Latest technology implementation: Most developers enjoy and look forward to working with the latest of technologies or methodologies. So it will be good information to share with the candidate if you, as the recruiter, know that the client has implemented any project using the latest technologies. The possibility of working with the best and latest technology is an attractive option for the candidate. Here is how you frame your question to receive the answer you seek.

CALL NOTES

"In terms of technology, what are the latest technologies your department has implemented in any of your projects? How deliberate are you in upgrading to the latest versions of software?"

Development tier: For the purpose of division of labor, application development can be divided into many layers, such as presentation, business logic, data access, and database. See Figure 1.3 for how these layers are separated. A key benefit of keeping these application layers separate is that it allows parallel development of the different tiers of the application. One developer can work on the presentation tier, while another builds the business tier, and another works on the database tier.

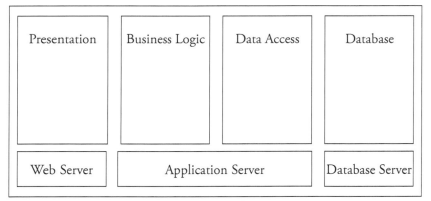

Figure 1.3. Multi-tier development.

Working on separate tiers also allows for less complicated maintenance and support, this is because it's simpler to change and upgrade a single specific component than to make changes in a one-tier application. If the business rules of a multitier application are changed, it's only necessary to change the software logic in the business tier on one server. With this in mind, seasoned developers prefer working on multitier applications, where every layer has been separated. It's easier to update and troubleshoot. So as a recruiter, you want to find out from the hiring manager (that is looking for a developer) the development tier in place in their organization. Here is how you frame your question to receive the answer you seek.

CALL NOTES

"In your development team, how do you separate the team members that work on a particular development tier? How many development tiers are present in your applications?"

Structured process or ad hoc-driven: Some technology organizations are more process driven than others; in these organizations, documentations are done and written processes are used for streamlining projects and for every change request. Some candidates would want to know if this is the case for the organization he is being recruited for. In my work experience as a developer, I thrived better when there was a set and known way to write code. This does not mean that one cannot deviate every once in awhile when there is a need for it, but it does mean that there is uniformity in how things are done, thus making it easy for the next developer to pick up where the other left off, with little wasted time. As a recruiter armed with this information alongside all the rest, you are able to keep your arsenal full with information, not only for this position but for this organization as a whole, making you the recruiter of choice for other requisitions that may arise from this company. Here is how you frame your question to receive the answer you seek.

CALL NOTES

"What is your process or standards for documentation, code generation, code review (peer-to-peer review of a developer's code), and version control? Do you have standards that everyone must follow, or is it a mixture of ad hoc and structured environment?"

Criteria for choosing one out of two: There are those occasions where all you have for a job requisition is one candidate; this question would definitely not work there. But the occasions where you have two to three good candidates for a job, you would want to know the hiring manager's criteria for choosing one person out of the two or three candidates presented. Whatever the answer is, it will help you fine-tune your search. Ultimately you want to save your client's time and make the choice easy for the manager by finding one or two great candidates where the hiring manager picks one of the two. The converse is to inundate the hiring manager with ten candidates, where she rejects nine out of the ten, resulting in diminished confidence in your abilities as the recruiter. Here is how you frame your question to receive the answer you seek.

CALL NOTES

"If you have two to three great candidates that fulfill your requirements, what would make you choose one over the other?"

Certifications or no certifications: As noted earlier in this chapter, there may be a specific reason why an organization requires certification, such as a partnership with a software vendor where the client organization is required to have one or two personnel with certain certifications. This is the case for Microsoft partnerships. Another reason may be that the client organization just wants to ensure that the candidate has done due diligence in a certain technical expertise. Speaking from experience, I have the Microsoft Certified Database Administrator MCDBA in SQL Server 2000 and the MCBMSP Microsoft Certified Business Management Solutions in Microsoft Dynamics CRM 4.0; these are tough exams to pass. The study and practice involved are painful, but I'm happy I did them because there are foundational skills I have from the process of training and studying for these exams that I probably would not have had otherwise. Having such certifications will show value proposition to organizations or a hiring manager, demonstrating the competency of the candidate.

Whatever the reasons are for an organization's need for certification, you would want to know these reasons. If there are no special reasons, then the job requisition may be better served if this requirement is removed. For candidates that have this certification, it's a foot in the door for them, but there are candidates who do not have the certification but have in-depth experience in all the other requirements who are really turned off by an organization's need for certification (for more on certifications, see Chapter Thirteen). Here is how you frame your question to receive the answer you seek.

CALL NOTES

"Is there a specific need for the certification requirement in your job description that I should know of? Do you need it to prove the competency of the candidate, or do you have a software vendor partnership requirement that will be fulfilled?"

Job Requisition—with All the Answers

With all the questions answered, you are now ready to create a customized job description. This description may form a part of the job description you post on Internet job boards or send to interested candidates. Whichever is the case, you have a job description different from the original and different from most recruiters that are engaged by the client for the same job. Your job description has more information, and it is information that's important in attracting the right kinds of candidates. See Figure 1.4 for a customized job description that includes more information for candidates.

SAMPLE

Senior .NET Developer (SharePoint)

We have a need for a highly skilled .NET Developer for our SharePoint deployment—which is a 5000+ user SharePoint environment with plans to continue growing. The primary focus for this position will be solution design, technology leadership, and application development in a SharePoint environment and other Microsoft and .NET technologies. The successful candidate will be responsible for gathering requirements, application design, database design, project team leadership, hard-core development, testing, and implementation.

You will be working for a consulting company with client engagements that range from Enterprise Portal implementations, Extranet implementations, new development, and 100% custom application development, to eCommerce, Business Intelligence, Data Warehousing, MS Dynamics CRM customizations, Enterprise Application Integration, and more. Applicants must have a strong background in a Microsoft development environment including Visual Studio.net, ASP.net, VB.net, C#, and MS SQL Server. Applicants must have excellent object oriented development skills, documentation skills, project management expertise, and maintain great professionalism.

Required Minimum Skills:
- Degree in the area of MIS, CIS, or Computer Science
- 5+ years minimum application development experience in a professional environment
- 1+ years of SharePoint experience (MOSS 2007)
- 2+ years of .Net application development
- 3+ years of MS SQL Server
- Database Design skills
- Object Oriented Design skills

Desired Experience:
- Experience with Silverlight, Dynamics CRM, BizTalk, or Commerce Server
- XML, XSL, ETL, Web Services, and SOA experience a plus
- Experience with Unified Modeling Language, Rational Methodology a plus
- MCSD not required but considered a plus

Figure 1.4. Customized job description.

Candidate Questions

From the review of the job requisition and the additional information received from the hiring manager, you are now able to draw up a list of questions that you will use to qualify and shortlist potential candidates for this job requisition. You may consider sharing this question list with the hiring manager; doing so ensures that you are on the same page with him and also creates the impression that you know your work. This further builds the hiring manager's confidence in your ability to find the right candidate for him. Sharing your questions may also encourage him to add other questions to your list. This assumes that you have found some candidate resumes that fulfill the main requirements in the job requisition. You are now about to call your candidates. Below is an illustration of your questions.

QUESTIONS

The recruiter may start by going through the preliminaries of basic recruiter and candidate greetings and afterward flow right into the interview.

Greeting:

Hello, Jim, my name is Nadine Clarke with ABC Consulting. I was referred to you by a mutual acquaintance (name the person if you have their permission) and wanted to speak with you about an opportunity that might interest you. Do you have a minute? (Get their permission to continue.)

Good, I have a .Net SharePoint development opportunity in Dallas, TX, that's looking for someone with your set of skills. It's for a consulting company with client deployments that ensure its employees are never bored. These deployments are for Enterprise Portal implementations, new development, custom application development, B2B eCommerce applications, Business Intelligence, Data Warehousing, Microsoft Dynamics CRM customizations, and Enterprise Application Integration.

I'm going to ask you a few questions if that is okay with you. (Get their permission to continue.)

1. *In your experience in .Net development, which development tier do you prefer to work with?*
2. *What does your average work week look like?*
3. *How many code cycles or prop cycles do you typically go through in a week or month? {follow-up-question}How would you change that if you could?*
4. *Which of the .NET components do you prefer to work with: C# or VB.Net or ASP.Net?*
5. *Tell me a little about your input in creating a process driven or methodology driven development environment, you know ... like documentation, code review process, unit testing, etc.*
6. *SharePoint is the main focus of development for this job. Would you mind sharing with me a customization or development project you've handled in the past on SharePoint? Please start with the problem and the process you went through to complete the project.*

For more specific questions on SQL Server, see Chapters Nine and Ten. In the next chapter we take a look at the candidate's resume in comparison with the job requisition in order to formulate more questions for the candidate.

Possibility Rating

With answers to the RFI from the hiring manager and also affirmative answers to the candidate questions from the candidate, the technical recruiter is well on the way to finding the best candidate for the .NET Developer (SharePoint) position.

Considering the candidate questions and the information from the RFI, Table 1.1 shows candidate answers that make for a good fit for this position.

Questions	Possible Answers
1. In your experience in .NET development, which development tier do you prefer to work with?	"I have worked on all the tiers at one time or the other—the presentation, business logic, data access, and database layers. Sometimes the layer I'm working on depends on the project—how familiar I am with the project and whether the project time frame allows for ramp-up time."
2. What does your average work week look like?	"On an average, I work 45 to 50 hours per week, sometimes less."
3. How many code cycles or prop cycles do you typically go through in a week or month? {follow-up-question}How would you change that if you could?	"We prop every Wednesday. For the type of environment and business we are in, I think that frequency is appropriate."
4. Which of the .NET components do you prefer to work with: C# or VB.Net or ASP.Net?	"I have experience on all of them, but C# is the one I work with most of the time."

Table 1.1. Possible candidate answers.

These questions are obviously only a subset of the questions that can be asked of a candidate based on the job description illustrated above. However. with the answers above, the possibility rating for this candidate may be between eighty to eighty-five over one hundred (85/100).

What We Learned

- When you review a job requisition, you should identify questions that you can ask of the hiring manager. These include questions about the platform, the network environment, the size of company or number of users, the current team if any, the level of expertise sought, and any skills mismatch.
- The Request for Information (RFI) is the list of questions directed at the hiring manager in order to gain clarification of any job description ambiguity and to confirm your understanding of the needs of the hiring manager.
- A customized job description different from the original was created from the answers received from the hiring manager and RFI.
- Candidate questions directed at validating the skills of the candidate were created. These questions were from the results of the answers from the RFI.

Chapter 2

The Technical Resume

In This Chapter

- Decipher the resume
- Correlation between the resume and the requisition
- Questions from a resume
- Going overboard—the recruiter's making

What is a resume, and why is it important? It's a candidate's product information, their brochure of services, their billboard, and the closest way a recruiter gets to know a person without actually meeting them. The resume can be an ally when written properly and can be an enemy of progress if written badly. As a recruiter you have probably seen hundreds of resumes and can readily rate them "good," "bad," and "ugly" at a moment's glance. There are some resumes that jump out at you saying "Look at me," and some that plainly just whisper, "You can pass me by now." When you look at a resume, there is some information you want to immediately see in the first page—information such as contact information, job title, summary of skills, and education.

In this chapter we break down a resume, making sure that all the parts that make up a resume are available, and we create questions from the resume; resumes almost always have unanswered questions when reviewed for a specific job requisition. We will also make the correlation between a resume and the job requisition and look for skills embellishments or "orphaned skills"—skills with no accompanying experience. Yes, a hiring manager may be happy to know that a candidate has experience in SharePoint Server, but he also wants to know where the candidate got that experience aside from their home server network.

In this chapter you will learn how to create verbiage or content for those skills that may have been omitted from the candidate's resume but of which the candidate actually has professional experience. This chapter will illustrate how this can be accomplished with authenticity.

Decipher the Resume

Reviewing a technical resume for a specific job requisition becomes easier when you have gone through Chapter One of this book, where the job requisition was reviewed, and the hiring manager has answered some questions about his needs in relation to the requisition. We will review the resume in Figure 2.1 for the .NET Developer—SharePoint Consultant position shown in Chapter One.

TIPS

Please note that some keywords are underlined to call your attention to them. We'll seek to find out more about the candidate's experience using the underlined skills.

SAMPLE

Steven Irmalaxi	
SharePoint Senior Consultant	

Steven's primary area of expertise is developing and implementing SharePoint collaboration portals and .NET web applications. He led the development of SharePoint Portal technologies for the ABC Company, Origins Inc., and RPI Inc. Functional areas of expertise are systems integration and architecture, enterprise collaboration data management, and information security.

Technical Skills Summary

O/S	Windows Vista, Microsoft Windows Server 2003, and Windows XP Professional
Languages	.NET(C#, VB and ASP), JAVA, XML, and SQL

Databases	SQL Server 2008, 2005, and 2000
Other	SharePoint 2007 and 2003, Team Foundation server, Visual Studio, Visual SourceSafe, Rational Suite, SharePoint Designer, Office 2003 and 2007

Professional Experience
ABC Consulting   June 2004–Present
Senior Consultant (SharePoint and .NET Developer)
- SharePoint developer for MOSS applications.
- Led the development for an Enterprise Content Management System utilizing MOSS and .NET technologies. The enterprise system will enable real-time collaboration across the multiple locations. SharePoint developer utilizing MOSS and InfoPath Forms Services.
- Developed critical data management systems for utilizing SharePoint 2007 and 2003 and other technologies to enhance functionalities.
- Developed the collaboration portal for the Office of Administration utilizing SharePoint 2003. It included integration with legacy systems and automating business procedures, alleviating the administrative burden of many of the current business processes and ensuring the security and quality of the data.

CXD Company   December 2003–April 2004
Senior Consultant (SharePoint and .NET Developer)
- Lead developer on the CXD Information Management System for the utilization of SharePoint 2003 and .NET custom web parts and applications.
- Developer for a customized project management system utilizing SharePoint portal and integrating it with .NET applications and Microsoft Project Server 2003.
- .NET software developer building custom web applications integrating into suite of tools that were displayed as a digital dashboard to the end user using SharePoint 2003 technologies. This was an all-encompassing system streamlining all business processes across the division.
- Lead developer for a web-based .NET application maintaining and coordinating domestic and international travel agendas, itineraries, and research.

Education
Bachelor of Science, Computer Information Systems, June 2003, New York State University.

> **Professional Certifications:** Microsoft Certified Solution
> Developer *MCSD.*

Figure 2.1. Sample SharePoint resume.

At first glance, it's easy to see that Steven has all the skills that are required for this position. It's a resume made in heaven for the SharePoint job requisition. But don't hurry to send Steven's resume to the hiring manager. Remember the questions about pace, average work week, and the type of company? All those answers need to be ascertained before you can say that Steven is a match for the hiring manager's company.

If the hiring manager's and Steven's answers look like the suitability matrix in Table 2.1, then you may reconsider Steve's suitability to this position.

Question	Hiring Manager	Steve
Type of company	Fast-growing IT consulting company.	Traditional company where he can learn and teach others, very family oriented.
Average week/pace	55+ hrs per week, sometimes more.	40 hrs/week, with the occasional two hours here and there.
Prop cycle	Twice a week, with one or two hot fixes per week.	Once in a month; on some occasions twice a month. Hot fixes are inevitable, but they are at the minimum.
Process	Have processes used maybe 65% of the time; sometimes the urgent need for a hot fix trumps the need to follow the process.	Process is utilized 90% of the time.

Table 2.1. Suitability matrix.

Steven is obviously not suitable for this position; other situations may influence him to accept this position, but he may not last more than a year in this company before he starts looking for another position more suitable for his lifestyle.

The bottom line when reviewing a resume for a match with a job requisition does not begin and end with technical skills. Yes, it may start with the technical skills, but other things are as important as the skills match. With all this in mind, let's take a look at the parts of this resume that include the candidate's overview, skills summary, education and certifications, and professional experience.

The candidate's overview: This is a summary of who the candidate is and what he's good at.

Skills summary: This section of the resume is like the glossary of skills terms, the nutshell overview of all the skills and technologies that this candidate has worked with. This is the portion of the resume that attracts the recruiter's eye, where the recruiter finds a list of all or some of the skills sought after.

Education and certifications: Education is important and usually found on the first page of the candidate's resume. Most technical jobs now require a minimum of a bachelor's degree, so it's important that the fulfillment of this requirement is placed on the front page.

Professional experience: Usually starts at the bottom of the first page and spans the rest of the resume pages.

Correlation between the Requisition and Resume

As a recruiter you may send a job description to a candidate requesting their resume in return. Some candidates may, upon reviewing the job description, update their resume to match the skills set on the job description. This is usually not an issue; sometimes it takes a job description to remind a candidate that she has experience in an area she may have omitted in her resume. When it becomes an issue is when you identify sprinkles of the skills in the job description but no experience to substantiate the skills.

Let's take a look at the job requisition presented in Chapter One, and compare it to two different resumes. One may have sprinkles of skills with no evidence of experience, while another has the skills backed up with experience. When reviewing a resume, it is not enough to accept the summary of skills (list of all technologies used by the candidate) as evidence of experience.

The technical recruiter should use the same summary of skills as a basis for an interview or conversation with the candidate. If a skills summary looks similar to an excerpt of Amber's resume, as shown below in Figure 2.2, with no references of the same skills in the professional experience section, then you must find out more.

SAMPLE

Amber Henderson
SharePoint Consultant

Amber has over twelve years experience in Information Technology, with seven years implementation and development experience with SharePoint as a subject matter expert.

Summary of Skills

SharePoint: Microsoft Office SharePoint Server 2007 (MOSS 2007), Windows SharePoint Services 3.0 (WSS 3.0), SharePoint Portal Server 2003, SharePoint Portal Server 2001, SharePoint Team Services

Programming: .Net: ASP.Net, C#, VB.Net, Web Services, SQL Server 2005/2008, Silverlight, CSS, XML, XSL, XSLT, Visual Studio 2005/2008

Platforms: Windows 2008/Vista/2003/XP/2000/NT, UNIX/Linux, HP-UX, DOS, Mac OS

Professional Experience

SharePoint Consultant ABC Company Inc 2002–2008

- Developed custom functionality with SharePoint 2007, implemented SharePoint for corporate intranet and collaboration.
- Created interactive web interface and was able to quickly add functionalities and reuse code.

Figure 2.2. Summary of skills sample
with no evidence of professional experience.

In finding out more, one of two things may occur: Amber does not have professional experience to back up the skills in the summary section, or she does but did not adequately include the experience in the professional experience section of her resume.

CALL NOTES

To find out more, you may ask questions like, "Please tell me more about your experience using C# or VB.NET for Web development. Feel free to use a problem and solution based scenario to describe how you used this skill."

TIPS

Please remember that it's not enough to create a summary of skills where you include all the skills the candidate says they have. You should always seek to substantiate those skills with actual experience.

Table 2.2 shows an example of what the responses may look like for each of the itemized skills. These answers can then be used to augment Amber's professional experience resume section and make it ready to be presented to the hiring manager.

Skills	Years	Candidate Response	Resume Update
.NET Development with C#, VB.NET, ASP.Net	5	"Needed to add a scheduling component on our online applicant tracking software ATS."	"Using ASP.Net, C#, and SQL Server, I was able to develop a solution that integrated seamlessly with current ATS."
Visual Studio .Net	5	"Used this since my early development days; there really wasn't a choice for me because that was the framework of choice for the company I worked for."	"It provided a framework to create applications that utilized Web services that were complementary to our current Web-based ATS application."

SharePoint	2	"Wanted to ensure that our organization's six regional offices were working with current versions of documentation."	"Implemented a document management and work flow application based on Microsoft Office SharePoint Server 2007. The solution reduced the volume and cost of handling paperwork by about 50 percent."
SQL Server/ Database Design	5	"Microsoft database solution is the default choice when working with Microsoft technologies. We needed a database management system for storing the ATS data."	"Using SQL Server 2000/2005, designed and implemented the database objects for the applicant tracking software."
Silverlight	1	"Wanted to develop a more interactive Web user interface for our ATS application built on the Microsoft .NET Framework."	"Taking advantage of the flexibility of Silverlight on .NET Framework, I was able to create an interactive Web interface and was able to quickly add functionalities and reuse code."
BizTalk	1	*"While working with a major bank who had partnered with another bank to provide back office capabilities to their customers, we needed a system to support reliable dataflow between the two organizations."*	*"We deployed Microsoft BizTalk Server 2006, Microsoft BizTalk Accelerator for SWIFT, and InfoPath Forms Services to provide interoperability with our bank and the partner bank."*

Table 2.2 Possible responses from candidate.

Adding Professional Experience

When reviewing resumes you may find that a candidate does have the experience but just omitted adding these hands-on experiences in the professional experience section of the resume. The technical recruiter is to do one of two things: either ask the candidate to update their resume to include the experience, or update the resume yourself to include the missing information using the responses received from the candidate during your conversation. Please seek to receive consent before and after you update or add to a person's resume. Using the responses from Table 2.2, the recruiter can update the candidate's resume to include the skills.

A sample resume after the recruiter update may look like the one in Figure 2.3. You will notice that in addition to referencing the skills sets—ASP. Net, C#, SQL Server 2005, Silverlight, and .NET Framework, we also added how these skills/tools were used.

SAMPLE

Amber Henderson
SharePoint Consultant

Amber has over twelve years experience in Information Technology, with seven years implementation and development experience with SharePoint as a subject matter expert.

Summary of Skills

SharePoint: Microsoft Office SharePoint Server 2007 (MOSS 2007), Windows SharePoint Services 3.0 (WSS 3.0), SharePoint Portal Server 2003, SharePoint Portal Server 2001, SharePoint Team Services

Programming: .Net: ASP.Net, C#, VB.Net, Web Services, SQL Server 2005/2008, Silverlight, CSS, XML, XSL, XSLT, Visual Studio 2005/2008

Platforms: Windows 2008/Vista/2003/XP/2000/NT, UNIX/Linux, HP-UX, DOS, Mac OS

Professional Experience

SharePoint Consultant   ABC Company Inc   2002–2008

- Developed custom functionality with SharePoint API that integrated seamlessly with current system using *ASP.Net, C#, and SQL Server 2005.*

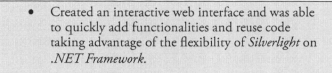

- Created an interactive web interface and was able to quickly add functionalities and reuse code taking advantage of the flexibility of *Silverlight* on *.NET Framework.*

Figure 2.3. Summary of skills sample with added professional experience.

Questions from a Resume

Aside from the usual nontechnical questions that arise from reviewing a resume, such as date discrepancies, years of experience for each skill, and why a candidate left their prior company, there are technical questions that may arise.

Looking at the SharePoint resume in Figure 2.1, the following are questions that a technical recruiter may ask a candidate that will give more insight to the candidate's experience. The recruiter may start the conversation like this after going through the preliminaries of the basic recruiter and candidate exchange.

"I'm going to ask you some general questions; your answers will give me a better understanding of what you do and perhaps what you enjoy the most in your job as a SharePoint Consultant. Is that all right?"

- "Tell me about the MOSS and .NET based Enterprise Content Management System—what problem did this solve? How long was the project? As a lead person, what would you have done differently to shorten the project time?"
- "As a lead role in this project, will you share the processes you went through to start and complete this project? What were the business considerations you made for some of the development work you did?"
- "How many other people were in your team? What were their roles?"
- "In addition to your development, testing, and production environments, did you also have staging and training environments? What role did the development team play in these other environments?"
- "What software did you use for version control? In these environments, who was responsible for moving the development

code from development to the testing environment? Was this person part of your team, too?"

- "What is the ratio of your lead role activities versus actual development: 50:50, 30:70, or what?"
- "How did you get into the SharePoint technology?"

Please wait for a response from your candidate before proceeding to ask another question.

TIPS

Skill Embellishments

Skill embellishment is the practice of including skills into a candidate's resume in order to match the job requisition. Seasoned technical persons with real-life professional experience will generally refrain from including skills in their resume of which they know little or nothing. The best practice for a technical recruiter is to avoid including skills in a candidate's resume unless the candidate has real-life work experience to back the skills up.

My colleague Mark once came out of an interview infuriated because he was sent there by a recruiter who had included many extra skills in the copy of his resume that was sent to the hiring manager. After spending a few minutes fielding questions of which he had little experience, he informed them that he had little interest in working as a database administrator.

He had thought the job was for a database engineer (see the difference between database administrator and database engineer in Chapter Ten). No wonder he was asked several questions on backup/recovery and other database administration questions. After the interview he requested to see the resume that was sent to the hiring manager; needless to say, it was weighed down with database administrator skills.

What We Learned

- The technical recruiter needs to decipher a technical resume to find out the suitability of a candidate to a job description.
- In reviewing the correlation between a resume and a job requisition, it is important to ask some simple questions, such as "tell me more about yourself." Answers to such questions have a way of bringing out more information about the candidate. This additional information can then be included in the candidate's resume.
- It is common for a technical recruiter to have to add professional experience when it has been omitted in the professional experience section of the resume.
- It is helpful to identify questions from a resume that give more insight to the candidate's experience.
- Avoid skill embellishment, which is the practice of including skills into a resume in order to match the job requisition, especially without the candidate's permission.

Chapter 3

Technology Team

In This Chapter

- Technology organizational chart
- Key role descriptions
- Recruiter's take

Whether you are a new technical recruiter or an experienced one, when introduced to a new client you immediately want to know more about the company, who the main contact person is, her counterparts, the makeup of her team, the role of the hiring manager, who she reports to, and who reports to her. In essence, you want to know more about your client.

In a technology group, there are many roles involved in the design, analysis, and implementation of a system. Software companies do not have typical IT departments in the real sense; this is because most aspects of jobs in this type of organization are technology based. Instead of the typical IT department, you find departments such as application development, database engineering, project management, and quality assurance—data warehouse departments where every main function is a full-fledged department complete with its own director and manager.

Nontechnology based companies have traditional IT departments, which report to either the Chief Finance Officer (CFO) or Chief Information Officer (CIO).

Technology Organizational Chart

Unless the roles played by people in a group are obvious, the recruiter should seek to understand the hierarchy of authority in each group. The natural inclination of most people after being introduced to a family is the need (albeit indirectly) to know who wields more authority in the relationship.

The technical recruiter should exercise this same inclination when faced with a new client. As the relationship between the recruiter and a company develops, the recruiter needs to figure out who reports to whom, where everyone fits, and factors affecting their decision to select a new hire. This information becomes crucial when the organization begins to decide on which of your candidates is the best fit for a position.

Using a pencil and paper and beginning with the CIO title is a good start in creating an organization chart for your new clients. As your relationship continues to grow, you can ask your contact hiring manager questions to find out who are the other influencers.

CALL NOTES

"Who else is involved with the hiring process in your group?"

"Is there anyone else with whom you would like me to discuss the job requirements?"

Armed with the information you collect during this process, you will know who has the last word, who the directors are, and who their direct reports are. The information you acquire here can help you create new relationships with other directors and managers who may also need your expertise in the future.

You may have created a perfect org chart for your client organization at one time or another, but it's important to keep one thing in mind: things change all the time, and people tend to move positions and companies. To ensure that the organizational chart you create stays relevant, it must include phone extensions, job titles, and first and last names. That way, when the inevitable change does come, the name may change but the title and phone extensions will most likely be retained.

Tech123.com (a dotcom company)

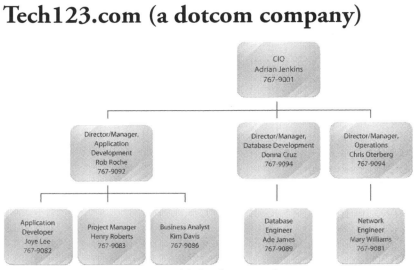

Figure 3.1. Technology org chart.

Figure 3.1 shows the organization chart for a typical technology consulting company specializing in implementing Microsoft business solutions for its clients. Here we review some job titles and roles as presented in the organization chart for the CIO, managers, business analysts, project managers, and developers involved in providing services to its clients.

CIO (Chief Information Officer)

Purpose: To provide knowledge of the existing IT environment and participate in architecting the environment required for all implementation projects.

Description: The CIO is responsible for the organization's entire IT environment, including all hardware and software set up in all possible locations within the organization. The CIO communicates regularly with the unit or department directors/managers during system analysis and the architecture design of any new hardware and software. The CIO has a good understanding of the organization and knowledge of the specific applications being used in the IT environment. The CIO is familiar with all the department heads and users who will be affected by any new implementation. The CIO should have a thorough understanding of the impact project decisions have on the IT infrastructure. This person acts as a resource to the directors.

Functional/Technical Skills: Detailed understanding of the technologies under his or her management and thorough knowledge of all the organization's related technologies. The CIO has fundamental understanding of all business systems within the organization. He or she has a good understanding of project methodology, business models, and data models for system implementation. The CIO has general IT knowledge and the ability to learn and understand new technologies.

Typical Activities: Reviews, approves, or disapproves all planning and proposal documents. Contributes to infrastructure analysis and design, and makes the decision on hardware and software within the organization. Supports decisions concerning business and financial aspects and also supports negotiation and finalization of contracting documents for any technical project implementation.

Director, Application Development

Purpose: To manage development managers and their staff, overseeing application development projects, providing mentorship and leadership to development staff.

Description: The person in this role has a breadth and depth of knowledge and experience in a wide range of application development methodologies, giving him or her ability to see the big picture in any development project and create development best practices. This person acts as a resource to managers.

Functional/Technical Skills: Demonstrated ability to lead multiple application development teams. Has demonstrated experience managing the support and enhancement of software, and is able to take ownership of multiple applications and accurately report schedules and status. With project management experience, the director of application development has the ability to manage and prioritize product requirements, including the ability to create accurate project plans. Has a good understanding of software architecture and the ability to work with lead engineers at a technical level to design flexible, scalable, and secure systems. Possesses good working knowledge of traditional and agile development methodologies. General knowledge of systems (e.g., various programming languages, databases, system and network architectures, design patterns, etc.). Web development experience is a plus, as is technical proficiency in the .NET + SQL Server, Java + MySQL, or other development framework plus database combination.

Typical Activities: Plans, leads, assigns, supervises, and controls activities related to software design and development. Oversees multiple software engineering teams and is responsible for the design and development of numerous products. Provides support to managers and their team members in order to meet organization's functional and quality requirements. Identifies and recommends technical options. The director role participates in the analysis and development of business requirements.

Director, Database Development

Purpose: Manages organization's database development. The director, database development oversees database development projects, creates best practices for database development, and acts as a support to database development staff.

Description: The director, database development oversees database engineers, data architects, and data analysts. This person also coordinates physical changes to databases, codes, tests, and implements numerous databases by applying knowledge of database management.

Functional/Technical Skills: The director of database development has thorough understanding and experience of database system operating characteristics, its capabilities, and limitations, and knowledge of the architecture, administration, infrastructure, and database systems tools. The director of database development has knowledge of multiple operating systems, such as Linux, UNIX, and Microsoft Windows. Has knowledge of the methodologies for data modeling in the design and creation of tables, relationships, indexes, unique constraints, and capacity requirements; is skilled in database performance tuning techniques, database security, and auditing functions. This person is also knowledgeable in client/server technology, architecture, software development life cycle, and other standards.

Typical Activities: Coordinates, supervises, and monitors the work of database developers. Plans and prepares performance reviews; hires and trains new personnel. Reviews and approves database management system configuration recommendations; oversees the development and organization of databases. This person recommends tools to assist in the management of the database development, testing, staging, and production environments.

The Director, Operations

Purpose: To manage technology operations, including the setup and implementation of hardware, network, and telecommunications infrastructure in an organization.

Description: The director of operations manages the configuration of network hardware and software, and the role also coordinates the implementation of security best practices and strategies. Production database administrators may often be found under the supervision and direction of the director of operations. This role communicates with the CIO and other business unit directors. The director of operations provides infrastructure technology vision to all business units and always seeks to provide cost-effective infrastructure solutions that reduce the total cost of ownership.

Functional/Technical Skills: The director of operations has thorough understanding of technology operations and best practices, and sound understanding and experience in contract negotiation and vendor management for software acquisition. Good knowledge of the system development life cycle and project management practices is also required. He or she is experienced in a broad range of applications, databases, and technologies areas, including enterprise systems, such as UNIX, AIX, Solaris, Linux, J2EE, and Windows Server; end user systems, such as desktops, laptops, and mobile devices; and global wide area network/ local area network related hardware and systems that connect different office locations. The director of operations has good experience in Systems Management and Information Security Operations, and managing implementation of operational tools and processes for Firewalls, IDSs, IPSs, VPN, and other security related technologies.

Typical Activities: Oversees the design and implementation of standards for local and wide area network infrastructure. Selects, evaluates, and hires personnel. Works with senior management to recommend and establish technology and business strategy. The director of operations manages vendor relationships to obtain best terms for the organization. Ensures budgets and schedules meet corporate requirements.

Business Analyst

Purpose: To review business processes in order to gain a complete understanding of current procedures, identify improvements, document those processes, and connect business people to information technology groups in an organization.

Description: The business analyst is responsible for analyzing and modeling existing business processes. The goal of business process analysis is to understand and document current business procedures and identify areas for improvement. A thorough understanding of the current state of the organization is necessary prior to recommending changes related to implementing a new business solution. The business analyst uses modeling tools to document the current state of business processes as well as the desired future state. The business analyst is responsible for the knowledge transfer of business implications to the application/database developers and project managers.

Functional/Technical Skills: The business analyst has business analysis skills and experience in modeling business processes, and has good documentation skills. She or he knows how to conduct workshops and training sessions and has good industry knowledge.

Typical Activities: The business analyst prepares for and conducts business process analysis, documents and presents analysis and modeling results, and transfers knowledge to application/database developers and project managers.

Project Manager

Purpose: Schedules and coordinates project resources and ensures that time and budget targets are being met.

Description: The project manager is responsible for ensuring that all aspects of a project are planned and executed in a manner that meets the implementation goals within an established time frame and budget. The project manager should have a thorough understanding of the product being developed, ensuring that all technical resource persons are performing within the established project plan.

Functional/Technical Skills: With a fundamental understanding of related technologies, the project manager has experience with the management of risk, change, issues, time, scope, resources, budget, and quality. Also has knowledge of methodology and best practices, and experience with Microsoft Office Project and/or other tools used for project management; has a good understanding of all major activities for a system development life cycle implementation, such as analysis, design, development, and deployment.

Typical Activities: The project manager scopes project phases, and identifies and acquires resources for a project. Conducts kick-off meetings, creates and maintains plans for all project activities, and participates in all application design and code review meetings. This is the go-to person for all project status communications related to the project. Ensures timelines are met and that the project is within budget; ensures deliverables are built according to specification and are finished on time.

Application Developer (Lead)

Purpose: To provide both technical and functional knowledge of the product being implemented and all related technologies required for the implementation.

Description: The application developer is the primary resource for determining the approach to be utilized in a project implementation. The application developer should possess a thorough understanding of the product from both a functional and technical perspective. He or she should have a comprehensive understanding of the implementation methodologies for the technology being utilized in product development, such as .NET or Java Framework. The lead application developer participates in every aspect of the development and implementation, working with business analysts to ensure full understanding of the change implications to current business processes. He or she designs and builds product deliverables according to specifications, escalates technical design or specification issues to business analyst/project manager and application development director, and works within a given time frame to complete coding. He or she follows good development practices and software development life cycle methodologies throughout product development.

Functional/Technical Skills: For a Microsoft Windows based company, the lead application developer should be knowledgeable in Microsoft .NET technology; Microsoft Visual Studio development system; hardware sizing and architecture; network and operating systems; server technologies—Microsoft SQL Server Database, Reporting Services, Analysis Services, N-tier architecture, and Web servers; and Internet technologies—Microsoft Internet Information Server (IIS), Microsoft BizTalk Server, and firewalls.

Typical Activities: Beginning phase includes estimations of technical and development tasks. Analysis phase includes analysis and validation of design. Design phase includes validation and review of design with peers and other developers for acceptance. Development phase includes the review of development and preparation for testing and deployment.

Why the Organization Chart

You may have experienced presenting a great candidate to a client who, after many interviews, turned your candidate down. The turndown may have been for many reasons, but one of the reasons may have been that the candidate did not meet a unique need of one of the key decision makers. For example, a member of the hiring team may have biases toward candidates with certifications. As a result, they will automatically reject resumes without such certifications. This type of information can be collected when using an organization chart to show who the key decision makers are and what unique criteria they may have beyond the technical requirements for the position.

You can use the organization chart to do several things, including identifying other potential clients within the organization, and finding out the influencers, directors, managers, and peers that play a part in deciding who is hired and why. The important thing is to ask the hiring manager the following questions:

CALL NOTES

"Who is the candidate's primary customer?"
"Who will participate in the interview? Are these managers or peers?" "Who else is involved in the selection process?"

The Recruiter's Take

There are many more titles and roles in a typical technology organization than are represented in Figure 3.1. The chart is only an example of what you may start with when creating the org chart of one of your clients. One of the objectives of the org chart is the ability to have a handle on who's who in an organization—their correct names, phone numbers, titles, and their ability to influence a decision.

There are simple ways to quickly create org charts. You can use Microsoft Word or PowerPoint, or your current ATS (Applicant Tracking System) might already have this functionality.

- Word/Presentation Application: Microsoft Word and PowerPoint 2007 come with an intuitive tool called *SmartArt* for quickly creating professional org charts. In either application, this tool is found in the *Insert Tab* under the Illustrations Group.
- Applicant Tracking System (ATS): Your company may already have an ATS that includes org chart creation. This process may work by requiring you to enter all the main contact persons in a certain client—CEO, CIO, HR Director, and Development Director, with the appropriate attributes like first and last name, title, department, phone, e-mail, etc. The ATS then creates an org chart based on the information entered for a particular client.

You might consider asking the hiring manager to send you their organization's chart. I must warn that most companies are reluctant to release their organization charts to recruiters for obvious reasons—employee poaching and unsolicited cold calls.

TIPS

Whatever you do, don't send your candidates a blank organization chart template requiring the candidate to complete their company's organization chart for you. This usually turns the candidate off from further dealings with the recruiter. Creating the org chart should really be the job of the recruiter.

What To Do with an Org Chart

Now that we've discussed the reason for the org chart and how to create one, let's move on to the things you can do with some of the contact information on the org chart.

- Invite the contacts to connect with you through LinkedIn.

- Ask your hiring manager for permission to meet with some of the high-level persons on the org chart or to set up a meeting where you meet with the other influencers.
- If you receive a negative response, then seek to learn as much as you can about the other employees, such as their past schools, what they consider a good fit, etc.

What We Learned

- The organization chart is an important tool in the recruiter's arsenal, helping the recruiter identify influencers at client organizations.
- In the study of a simple organization chart, we reviewed the job roles of the following titles:
  o CIO: Responsible for the overall IT outlook in the organization and provides overall IT direction.
  o The Director, Application Development: Manages development managers and their staff, overseeing application development projects, and providing mentorship and leadership to development staff.
  o The Director, Database Development: Manages organization's database development. Oversees database development projects, creates best practice for database development, and acts as a support to database development manager and staff.
  o The Director, Operations: Manages technology operations, including the setup and implementation of hardware, network, and telecommunications infrastructure in an organization.
  o Project Manager: Identifies and manages the project team, ensuring that timelines are met and that the project is within budget.
  o Business Analyst: Reviews business processes to gain a complete understanding of current procedures; documents those processes and identifies improvements.
  o Application Developer (Lead): Provides both technical and functional knowledge of the product being implemented and all related technologies required for the implementation.

- Simple ways to quickly create org charts include using Microsoft Word, PowerPoint, and your current ATS (Applicant Tracking System).
- We also discussed why the organization chart is important in discovering influencers and their decision-making process during candidate selection.

SECTION TWO

Chapter 4

Networking Fundamentals

In This Chapter

- From the beginning
- Open Systems Interconnection (OSI)
- Categories of networks
- Types of networks
- Network protocols

From the Beginning

Why would a technical recruiter care about networking? Anyone in an office environment in this day and age understands to a certain degree the importance of interconnectivity to other computers and the Internet.

Computers can accomplish little without the ability to network with other computers and peripherals. The power of networking lies in its ability to connect with other computers without barriers, to send and receive information to and from others, and to share resources with others.

If you take a look at software applications or computer hardware devices, you will find that almost all of them have some form of networking capability. Networking enables computer users to share resources in order to save cost. Without a network, imagine purchasing a printer or scanner for every computer in your company or home. Some uses of networking include: file sharing, where files can be stored in a central location so that other users are able to access them; printer sharing, where a printer can be shared by multiple users, thereby saving the cost of purchasing individual printers and the space to locate them; and communicating through the network using mail services.

This chapter describes the types and uses of a network and the components and protocols that make up a network. The chapter also demonstrates the flow of information through a network and the protocols involved in each stage.

The Open Systems Interconnection (OSI) Network Model

In order to understand the fundamentals of networking, the technical recruiter needs to know the different layers of networks, the protocols found in each layer, and how these layers interact with each other. The OSI Model defined by the International Standards Organization (ISO) is a classification of network communication as a series of layers. It describes how the network layers interact with each other.

Seven Layers of the OSI Network Model

There are seven layers in this model: application, presentation, session, transport, network, data link, and physical. These layers have been described using communication between two users and the pictorial representation of how data moves from one network layer to the other.

o   The Application Layer provides connection to a network using applications. The Outlook e-mail application and database queries are examples of applications in this layer.

o   The Presentation Layer takes the data from the application layer and presents it in a format that is understandable by computers. This layer also encrypts/compresses data on the origination layer and decrypts/decompresses data on the destination layer.

o   The Session Layer opens and closes sessions between two computers during communication.

o   The Transport Layer breaks down data into manageable segments and delivers them error free and in a proper sequence.

o   The Network Layer routes messages and data to the appropriate address by the best available path.
o   The Data Link Layer identifies the recipient computer on the network; this layer controls who has access to the physical network, eliminating possible confusion over the ownership of data.
o   The Physical Layer is the actual physical connection between the computers. Devices such as hubs, routers, cables, and network adapters operate in this layer.

To describe the OSI model, we use an illustration of a typical noncomputer network communication between two users. Katie is the originator, and Donna is the recipient of Katie's message.

o   Kate types a document.
o   Kate puts it in an envelope, addresses it, and leaves it for mail pickup.
o   The mail clerk picks up the envelope and delivers it to the mail room.
o   The mail room staff reads the address and determines how to route the mail.
o   After determination, the staff places the envelope inside another envelope,
o   And arranges for pickup.

The envelope goes through transport to the intended recipient in the following fashion.

o   The envelope is delivered in the mail room of Donna's office.
o   The mailroom staff removes the outer envelope.
o   They determine who the mail is for and sorts it for delivery.
o   A mail clerk takes the mail to Donna's office and delivers the mail with the others sorted for the same recipient.
o   Donna opens the mail and reads it.

Now look at a typical network communication between the same two people (see Figure 4.1).

o   The transmission starts when Kate types an e-mail message to Donna and presses the "send" key; this occurs in the Application Layer.

o   Kate's operating system appends to the message a packet (envelope) that identifies the sender and intended recipient(s); this occurs in the Presentation Layer.

o   The message is translated in a format that will be understandable by computers; this occurs in the Presentation Layer.

o   The message is then prepared for transmission and transport; this occurs in the Session, Transport, Network, Data Link, and Physical Layers.

o   Adding delivery and reading of the message completes the journey of Kate's e-mail.

The sequence of events for message delivery through a network is similar to a person-to-person communication. At each stage, header information is attached to the sent data and then stripped as it goes down the recipient's protocol stack.

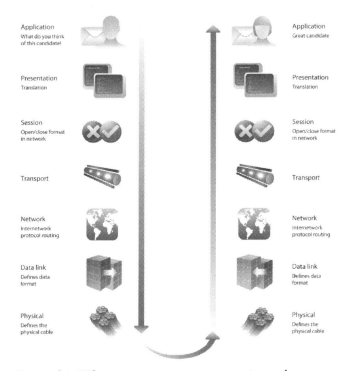

Figure 4.1. When two computers communicate, data passes up through the sender's protocols, across the network, and then down the recipient's protocol stack.

Definition of Server and Client

A client is a computer or application that receives information or resources from another computer. When a computer is making a request to another computer, the requesting computer is referred to as a client.

The server is a program or computer system that responds to and fulfills requests from client computers in a networked environment. When a computer is fulfilling a request, it is serving, and therefore is referred to as a server. In some cases, computers can act as both a server and a client, making requests of other servers (as a client) and also fulfilling requests from other servers (as a server).

Figure 4.2. Network connections.

The client and server computers are connected using network media such as cables, fiber-optics, or wireless networking interfaces between the computer systems. The network adapter is the physical piece of hardware that allows your computer to connect to a network. Whether the network media is cable, fiber optics, or wireless, the physical connection that we usually see is called a network adapter. For wireless network connections, this will be the wireless network card or wireless adapter.

Categories of Networks

Computer networks can be either peer-to-peer networks or server-based networks.

Peer-to-Peer Networks

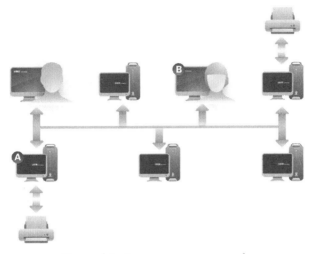

Figure 4.3. A peer-to-peer network.

This is a type of network where each computer acts as either a server (responding to requests) or a client (requesting resources) or both. There is usually no centralized control of resources in this type of network.

Pros

o   Setup is fairly easy where all computers are linked together.

o   Inexpensive because there is no need to purchase a separate network operating system or a server computer.

o   Easier to maintain because there is little or no network configuration that may require technical expertise beyond the basic information contained in the instructions that come with the purchased hardware.

Cons

o   There is a known decrease in the performance of computers that perform the role of a server in a peer-to-peer network.

o   Security is weak in this scenario. Users are not required to provide any credentials to log in or use network resources.

o   Decentralized resources could be difficult to manage. You
     will notice in Figure 4.3, that as a result of having a printer
     on computer (A), the person at computer (B) may not have
     access to printing when computer (A) is shut down.

Server-Based Network (Client/Server)

A server-based network is a network of computers that have a computer
dedicated as a centralized controller of all the network resources. In
a server-based network, the centralized computer is usually more
sophisticated in terms of the internal processing resources it requires to
satisfy requests generated by clients. It requires a Network Operating
System (NOS), such as Windows Server 2003/2008 or UNIX. With the
network operating system, users are configured in a domain structure
requiring user names and passwords to gain access to the network.

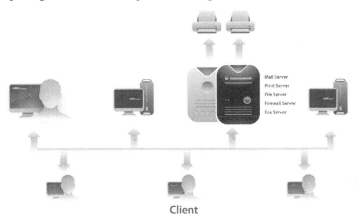

Figure 4.4. A server-based network, where the
server resources are centrally controlled.

Pros

o   Security is controlled in a central location/server.
o   Faster access to network resources; this is because the server
     has more processing power.
o   The server is always on, and this ensures that resources are
     always available.

Cons

o   More expensive to implement a network; may require a
     systems administrator.

o   Involves network and user access configuration; therefore, is more complicated than the peer-to-peer network.
o   Requires the purchase of a network operating system (NOS).
o   Requires more expensive server hardware.

Types of Networks

There are two main types of networks: local area networks and wide area networks.

Local Area Networks (LAN)

A Local Area Network (LAN) is a computer network covering a small geographic area, like a home, or one location, such as an office or school. With LANs, there are wired and wireless networks. LAN technologies function at all the layers of the OSI reference model.

Wired Local Area Network

In a wired LAN environment, the connection of local computers on a network is done through the use of cables or wires.

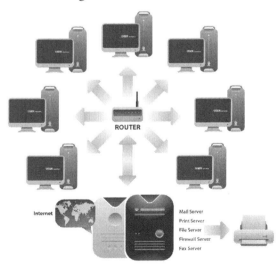

Figure 4.5. Wired LAN structure.

Pros

  o   Security: it's more difficult to break into the wired network than the wireless network.

  o   Speed: the speed on the wired network is usually faster than the wireless.

  o   Reliability: wired networks have relatively stable network connectivity. It's unusual to experience dropped connectivity unless the cable is unplugged or you encounter other issues that may not be related to the reliability of the wired network.

  o   Cost: if a home or office is prewired, then it is considered an easy installation.

Cons

  o   Cost: in instances where the office needs to install new network jacks, the cost of ownership is higher than the wireless network.

  o   Setup: may require the hiring of a technician to run wires and cables and configure the network and security.

  o   Immobility: users on a wired network have limited mobility.

Wireless Local Area Network

The wireless LAN is the connection of local computers on a network without the use of cables or wires. This is typical in homes because it's easier to install or in offices where employees who are always in and out of meetings need access to their computers. Some of these same offices may also have a combination of the wired and wireless networks, where each network (wired or wireless) has a purpose to fulfill.

Figure 4.6. A wireless peer-to-peer network.

Pros

  o   Cost: because of the ease in installation (does not require breaking walls or mounting wall jacks), the total cost of ownership of a wireless network compared to the wired may be less expensive.

o   Easy setup: when installation directions are followed, it is easier to install in homes or small offices, and therefore it may not require a support person.

o   Mobility: users on a wireless network are able to move from room to room with their computers (usually laptops) with ease.

Cons

o   Lack of security: it's easier to break into a wireless network than the wired.

o   Slow speed: the speed on the wireless networks is usually lower than the wired.

o   Unreliability: as a result of the nature of the wireless technology, which is on a radio frequency, there are higher rates of dropped network connectivity.

Wide Area Networks (WAN)

A WAN is a data communications network that is geographically separated. WAN technologies are mostly found to function at the lower three layers of the OSI reference model: the physical layer, the data link layer, and the network layer.

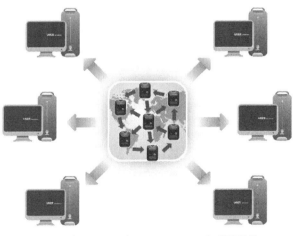

Figure 4.7. A Wide Area Network (WAN).

WANs are mostly used by organizations that have multiple office locations, requiring a secure and cost-effective network solution for their employees to communicate and share information across a network. WANs are used for centralized merchant transactions in retail or hospitality businesses and can also be used for secure access to remote but internal organization software applications such as timesheet or human resources software. Wide Area Networks can either be private or public and wired or wireless, and can be implemented using technologies such as remote access VPN or point-to-point connections.

Point-to-Point Connection

A point-to-point connection provides a single WAN communications path from one location to a remote network through a carrier network, such as a telephone company.

Figure 4.8. Point-to-point connection through a WAN to a remote network.

Point-to-point lines are usually leased from a telephone company and are seen as dedicated lease lines. Point-to-point connections are more expensive than shared services. Figure 4.8 illustrates a typical point-to-point connection through a WAN.

Virtual Private Network (VPN)

The function of VPN is to allow two computers or networks to talk to each other over a nonsecure Internet connection. VPNs rely on tunneling to create a private network; tunneling is the process of placing a data packet within another packet and sending it over a network. Figure 4.9 illustrates a remote access VPN connection.

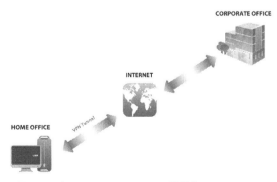

Figure 4.9. A remote access VPN connection.

Though VPNs offer a WAN connectivity through Internet networks at greatly reduced operating costs, the reduced costs are accompanied by increased security risks. VPN security depends on a number of factors, such as type of client-server systems (Windows, UNIX, etc.), level of security, and network resources accessed.

Network Protocols

Protocols are sets of rules that manage network communications between two computers. Listed below are some protocols you may have seen on some job descriptions and what they do. There are also protocols known as connection and connectionless protocols.

Connection communication is similar to what happens when you make a telephone call: the call is initiated, connection is established, you speak with a person at the other end, and then the connection is terminated when the conversation is ended. This type of connection is used in WAN environments where there needs to be an established connection between two or more devices—referred to as a handshake.

Connectionless communication is similar to sending a piece of stamped (with no upgrade options) mail through the regular post office, where you do not know exactly when the mail will arrive nor receive any acknowledgement that it was received. This type of connection is used in LANs through the User Datagram Protocol UDP for sending streaming audio or video messages.

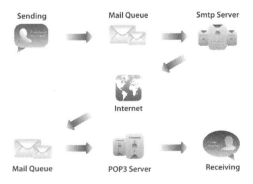

Figure 4.10. Connectionless communication.

Below are descriptions of networking protocols used in networks today.

o   IP: The most widely used, the Internet Protocol, handles all network addressing in a TCP/IP network. IP provides connectionless datagram service for fast but unreliable communication between computers. IP is discussed further in the section below.

o   TCP: Transmission Control Protocol is the primary transport layer protocol.

o   FTP: File Transfer Protocol provides a method for transferring files between computers.

o   Telnet: An Internet protocol that allows you to connect your PC as a remote workstation to a host computer anywhere in the world and use that computer as if it were local. Telnet allows terminal emulation, which is the ability to access a remote computer and use its resources.

o   SMTP: Simple Mail Transfer Protocol is a TCP/IP protocol used in the process of sending and receiving e-mail.

o   UDP: User Datagram Protocol provides a connectionless transportation service on top of the Internet Protocol (IP).

o   ARP: Address Resolution Protocol maps hardware address to IP address for delivery of data on a local area network.

o   SNMP: Simple Network Management Protocol allows network administrators to connect to and manage network devices.

o   PPP: Point-to-Point Protocol provides dial-up networked connection to networks. PPP is commonly used by Internet Service Providers (ISPs) as the dial-up protocol for connecting customers to their networks.

o   POP3/IMAP: Post Office Protocol/Internet Message Access Protocol are ways for client computers to connect to mail servers and collect e-mail.

The IP Language

Just as we need a common language in which to communicate with each other, computers in a network environment need and have a language of communication; it's IP—Internet Protocol. M. J. Norton in *IP as a Second Language* refers to IP as the universal language in networking. The IP is the most popular nonproprietary protocol suite because it can be used to communicate across any set of interconnected networks and is well-suited for LAN and WAN communications.

The Internet protocols consist of a suite of communication protocols, of which the two best known are the Transmission Control Protocol (TCP) and the Internet Protocol (IP). The Internet protocol suite is used for common applications, such as electronic mail, terminal emulation, and file transfer. This section discusses the IP suite because it is the most used protocol in networking.

Since its early development thirty years ago, Internet protocols have since become the foundation on which the Internet and the World Wide Web (WWW) are based. You will find IP addresses in every network device no matter the size or type of network, whether home, company LAN, or the Internet. In order for any computer to connect with another, it requires an IP address. This address makes it possible for a UNIX or MAC machine to communicate with a PC.

Types of IP Addresses

There are two basic types of IP Addresses: static and dynamic IP addresses.

A static IP address is a number that is permanently assigned to a certain computer and does not change. Once a computer has been assigned its IP address, it will keep it indefinitely. The advantage of a static IP address is that the computer will always have the same IP address on the network and will be easy to identify in the future once its IP address is known.

A dynamic IP address is a number that is assigned to different computers at different times. This means that every time a computer is connected to a network, it is assigned a random IP address from a pool of IP addresses depending on IP availability. For example, if your company network uses dynamic IP addresses, it means that when you start your computer and it wants to log into the network, it will get a new IP address.

What We Learned

- The OSI Model defined by the International Standards Organization (ISO) is a definition of network communication as a series of layers and describes how the network layers interact with each other. There are seven layers in this model: application, presentation, session, transport, network, data link, and physical.

- A client is a computer or application that receives information or resources from another computer, typically known as a server.
- The server is a program or computer system that responds to and fulfills requests from client computers in a networked environment.
- Two categories of networks are peer-to-peer networks and server-based networks.
- The two main types of networks are Local Area Network (LAN) and Wide Area Network (WAN). A Local Area Network is a computer network covering a small geographic area, like a home, or one location, like an office or school, while Wide Area Networks cover geographically separated areas. Network Protocols are sets of rules that manage network communications between two computers.
- The Internet Protocol is the most popular nonproprietary protocol suite because it can be used to communicate across any set of interconnected networks and is appropriate for LAN and WAN communications.

Chapter 5

Operating System Fundamentals

In This Chapter

- Overview of operating systems
- Capabilities of the operating system
- Server operating systems versus desktop operating systems
- Skills sets required for operating systems administrators
- How to read candidate resumes and certifications

In this chapter, the computer operating system is introduced and then expanded with details of the types and uses of each operating system. Every computer system needs an operating system. Understanding the difference in operating systems and how to spot the perfect candidate to support or administer each adds to the technical recruiter's success.

Using the find and replace tool found in word processors, it's now very easy for one person to copy another person's resume by swapping contact details and company names of the original resume owner with theirs. Thus it's become imperative for a technical recruiter to speak at length with a candidate to understand the candidate's experience and skills. It's no longer adequate to weigh the number of times a keyword appears on a resume or approve a candidate as suitable because all the keywords in a job description are found on the candidate's resume.

What Is an Operating System?

An *operating system* (O/S) is software that controls the resources on a computer system, how other programs or software behave on the computer, and the overall management of a computer system's resources. For instance, the management of input and output resources, memory allocation, job scheduling, system boot, and recovery are all managed by the operating system.

The O/S is the first program loaded on a computer system that provides an interface between the computer's hardware, software, and the user. Figure 5.1 illustrates the interface of the hardware to the operating system, the operating system to the application, and then the application to the user.

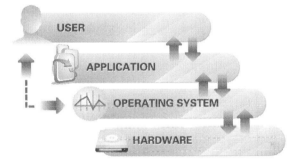

Figure 5.1. Operating system interface with hardware, software, and user.

Every application that runs on the computer is a result of how the operating system interfaces with the hardware and human operators. In the simplest terms, the operating system is the middleman between your computer's hardware and yourself. This includes hardware such as the mouse, keyboard, wireless card, and memory. In the past, there used to be operating systems that were not network capable; now, however, almost every commercial operating system has the ability to connect to local and wireless networks. Figure 5.2 illustrates further how the operating system is the center of attention for every other application software or hardware device installed or connected to the O/S.

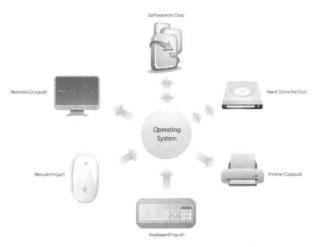

Figure 5.2. Operating system as the middleman between input/output hardware and software.

Capabilities of the Operating System

Among the main capabilities of the O/S are its ability to *multitask*, its ability to provide *networking* between the hosting computer and other computers and peripheral devices, and its ability to *secure* the contents of the hosting computer. Other operating system tasks are processor, memory, device, and storage management.

- Multitasking is a method by which operating systems handle multiple tasks from the same or multiple software applications.
- Networking is the ability for an operating system in one computer to connect to another in order to share resources or respond to requests made by another computer.
- Security is the ability for an operating system to protect its host computer from deliberate attacks.

Categories of Operating Systems

There are two main types of operating systems: the *desktop operating system*, which may be referred to as a single user operating system; and the *network operating system*, which is a multiuser operating system. The differences between desktop and network operating systems vary to a certain degree, and the variance really depends on the need and use in a given environment. The desktop operating systems are the types used on our desktop and laptop computers. The network operating systems are the types installed on server computers.

Some software applications require that they be installed on server operating systems because of the capacity and processing power found in the hardware that hosts the network operating systems. The everyday user may not need a network operating system unless that user is a developer who needs to build applications that run on server operating systems and thus requires the use of the server O/S.

Table 5.1 lists some examples of server applications and their operating system requirements. As shown, Microsoft Exchange Server (Microsoft's e-mail and collaboration software) runs only on the Windows Server operating system and does not work with UNIX or Linux (at least at the time of this writing). Oracle Database Server (Oracle's database software), Microsoft SQL Server (Microsoft's database software), and SAP CRM (SAP's customer relationship management software) have the ability to work under the Windows, Linux, or UNIX operating systems.

Server Applications	Windows Server	Linux	UNIX
Microsoft Exchange Server	✓		
Microsoft SQL Server	✓		
SAP CRM	✓	✓	✓
Oracle Database Server	✓	✓	✓

Table 5.1. Server applications and the Network O/S they work with.

Desktop Operating Systems

A desktop operating system is the operating system found on client or end-user computers, such as Windows XP, Vista, and Windows 7. When a computer in a network has a server that controls its access to network resources and security, that server is loosely known as the domain controller. This domain controller controls how and if a desktop computer joins the network, prints, browses the Internet, and shares other network resources.

The desktop O/S does not have as much processing power as the server operating systems. When a desktop is on a network that does not have a domain controller, then this desktop is a king unto itself, controlling its access to all resources available to it.

Examples of other desktop operating systems are Apple—OS 9.1, Apple—OS X Snow Leopard, Sun Microsystems—Solaris 10, and Linux.

Network Operating Systems

The Network Operating System (NOS) is an operating system installed on a computer identified as a server in a client-server network environment. It controls the network, the resources on the network, and desktop computers attached to the same network as the server computer. The network operating system communicates through Local Area Networks and Wide Area Networks to allow users to share files, disks, printers, and other network resources.

It provides data integrity and security by allowing and restricting access to certain resources and files. The NOS utilizes administrative tools for adding, changing, and removing users, computers, and peripherals from the network. The NOS also has troubleshooting tools that inform network administrators of network activities. The NOS includes internetworking support that ties multiple networks together and provides file and print sharing, user account administration, and network security.

Examples of network operating systems are Microsoft Windows Server NT 2000/2003/2008, SUSE Linux Enterprise Server 10, MAC OS X Snow Leopard Server, HP UNIX—11i, Sun Solaris 10, Red Hat Enterprise Linux Advanced Platform, and IBM AS/400.

Operating System Types

You can probably tell the type of network your client has by looking at a job requisition. If the job description is requesting Linux or UNIX skills, then the client is a UNIX/Linux shop. The same is true for Windows. That's as simple as it gets. Now there are environments that are combined, where the environment runs both the Windows and UNIX/

Linux operating systems based on the software application needs of the organization and the perceived strengths of each operating system.

The manufacturers of the network operating systems listed in Table 5.2 compete for the same organizations and thus include mostly the same functionalities for networking, security, file sharing, and disk and storage management. Operating systems fall under UNIX, Linux, Windows, Macintosh, and Mainframe categories. Table 5.2 lists some of the major network operating systems, manufacturers, and their latest releases as of the time of this writing.

Name	Manufacturer	Flavor	Release
AIX	IBM	UNIX	Version 6.1
HP—UX	Hewlett-Packard	UNIX	Version 11i v3
Mac OS X Server	Apple Inc.	UNIX	Version 10.6 Snow Leopard
Solaris	Sun Microsystems	UNIX	Version 10 5/09
Windows Server	Microsoft	Windows	Windows Server 2008
z/OS	IBM	Mainframe	Version 1 Release 11
Red Hat Linux	Red Hat	Linux	Enterprise Linux 5
SUSE Linux	Novell	Linux	SUSE Linux Enterprise 11

Table 5.2. Network operating systems.

UNIX

Each operating system has its strengths. UNIX is strong in its ability to be uncompromised by viruses, hacking, and security breaches. This is the reason some organizations that implement the Windows operating system utilize UNIX or Linux as the operating system installed on their firewall server. There are many flavors of the UNIX operating system, and the following section reviews the IBM AIX, HP—UX, and Sun Solaris flavors, as well as the Mac OS X Server.

IBM's AIX: IBM's UNIX-based operating system includes functionalities such as system management, security, availability, and virtualization. This operating system supports 32- and 64-bit applications. AIX only operates on IBM hardware systems—IBM UNIX operating system based servers. AIX provides a System Management Interface Tool (SMIT) referred to as "smitty," used for system administration.

HP—UX: HP's 64-bit UNIX-based operating system functions with virtualization, system management, security management, clustering, file system management, developers' tools, and partitioning. Because the HP Company is a software company as well as a hardware manufacturing company, the HP—UX operating system only operates on HP hardware servers; the plan is for organizations to purchase both the operating systems and server hardware. HP—UX provides the System Administration Manager (SAM) as a tool used for system administration.

Sun Solaris: Created by Sun Microsystems, its latest release is the v10 5/09, with features that include security, performance, networking, data management, interoperability, virtualization, availability, and platform choice (the ability to select a server hardware of choice for installation). Sun Solaris UNIX-based operating system can be installed on other manufacturers' server hardware, such as Dell.

Mac OS X Server: Created by Apple Computers, the Mac OS X Server is built on the UNIX operating system foundation. It looks similar to MAC desktops in its simplicity of use but comes with more operating power since it's obviously a server operating system. The Mac OS X Server comes bundled with server applications, such as e-mail, collaboration, calendaring, and chat applications. Just like other Apple products, the Mac OS X Server delivers rich graphics.

Linux

Linux operating system is increasing in popularity, and Linux is becoming available on many server platforms. Both Red Hat and Novell SUSE Linux are platform insensitive. This means that they can run on as many hardware server computers as possible from DELL, IBM, and HP, to even high-powered personal computers. The ability of the Linux operating system to run on inexpensive hardware and the large number of developers involved in the development of Linux are increasing the widespread use of Linux as the development platform of choice for new business applications.

Red Hat Linux: Created by the Red Hat company, this operating system comes in both server and desktop versions. It's not hardware specific and is also available for mainframe computers. Reasons why organizations both big and small are turning to Red Hat and other Linux-based operating systems include reduced total cost of ownership, the availability of thousands of certified software applications that run on this O/S, open source technologies, and interoperability with other Unix software.

Novell SUSE Linux: Owned by Novell and similar to Red Hat, Novell SUSE Linux is not hardware specific and is available in both server and desktop versions. SUSE includes functionality such as virtual machine management tools, and support for .NET applications on Linux. Many software application companies are getting their software certified as Certified Software Applications on SUSE Linux.

Windows

Windows was created by Microsoft and is available in both desktop and server versions. The Windows server operating system's latest version is the Windows 2008 64-bit version. There is yet another category of the Windows server referred to as the Windows Small Business Server (SBS), which comes bundled with Exchange Server for e-mail, SharePoint Services for collaboration, and SQL Server for database. The Windows SBS is used in small organizations with a maximum of seventy-five users. Similar to other server operating systems, the Windows 2008 server operating system functionalities include system management, active directory management, virtualization, Web server, networking security, and storage management.

Mainframe

In Introduction to the New Mainframe: z/OS Basics by IBM Redbooks, it's noted that a mainframe is the central data repository in a corporation's data processing center, linked to users through less powerful devices such as workstations or terminals. The presence of a mainframe often implies a centralized form of computing, as opposed to a distributed form of computing. You may wonder why mainframe technology attracts very little attention even in the IT field. John Kettner, one of the coauthors of this book, wrote in August 2009:

"That this is so is perhaps not surprising. After all, who among us needs direct access to a mainframe? And, if we did, where would we find one to access?"

Mainframes tend to be hidden from the public eye and are highly resistant to most forms of abuse that badly affect personal computers, such as e-mail-borne viruses and Trojan horses.

IBM z/OS: The z/OS mainframe operating system is manufactured by IBM, and its latest release is Version 1 Release 11. It's the most widely used and advertised mainframe operating system from IBM. It functions as a central repository to keep applications and data available and secure.

Operating System Skills Sets

As a technical recruiter, one should be cognizant of the fact that just because a candidate has had the opportunity to work in a high-profile network environment and has become familiar with the environment does not mean that the candidate has the required skills set or that the candidate actually implemented or supported the network.

When recruiting operating system administrators, recruiters need to understand how an operating system skills set supports an organization's IT infrastructure. The most common operating systems are mainframes, UNIX, Linux, and Windows. In the following section are the most common skills sets sought after for managing and supporting each operating system.

Windows Skills Sets

The skills sets you see in a Windows Administrator candidate resume or job description requirement include managing the hardware and software components, the users in the network, the security, and the file system. Every Windows Administrator must have good skills in these areas, and should be able to answer questions on how he/she configures and performs troubleshooting activities on these tools. We discuss the questions to ask candidates in a later section.

RESUME PHRASES   Windows System Administrator

Active directory administration, domain trusts administration, DHCP, DNS, organizational units (OU), TCP/IP, OSI Model, group policy, LAN security, IIS, WINS, SMTP.

Figure 5.3. Phrases in a Windows System Administrator's resume.

Active Directory (AD): The directory service stores information about objects on a network and makes this information available to users and network administrators. AD gives network users access to permitted resources anywhere on the network using a single log-on process. It provides network administrators with an intuitive, hierarchical view of the network and a single point of administration for all network objects.

Active Directory Users and Computers is an administrative tool used in performing the day-to-day administrative tasks of managing network users, their computers, security, and user access to resources. The Windows system administrator should know how to use AD to create, delete, modify, move, and set permissions on objects stored in the directory. The Windows systems administrator should also have experience creating and configuring AD objects such as organizational units (OU), users, contacts, groups, computers, printers, and shared file objects.

Internet Information Server (IIS): Software service that supports Web site creation, configuration, and management, along with other Internet functions. Internet Information Server includes Network News Transfer Protocol (NNTP), File Transfer Protocol (FTP), and Simple Mail Transfer Protocol (SMTP). IIS has many tentacles. With the advancement of Web-based programming, software manufacturers are creating Web-based counterparts of their applications, and as a result, IIS with its Web configuration function is utilized in most Web-enabled applications created by Microsoft. Applications like Microsoft SQL Server Reporting Services, Dynamics Customer Relationship Management, FTP, SMTP, and WWW publishing are all examples of tools that require IIS to function. Therefore, this makes IIS an important tool for every Windows system administrator to understand and have the ability to configure and manage.

Simple Mail Transfer Protocol (SMTP): SMTP is a member of the TCP/IP suite of protocols that governs the exchange of electronic mail between message transfer agents. It transports electronic mail through a network. A Windows Administrator worth his pay should know the inner workings of this protocol and how to configure it in a network environment.

Dynamic Host Configuration Protocol (DHCP): This is a TCP/IP protocol that dynamically leases IP addresses to network client computers. DHCP uses a client/server model where the DHCP server maintains centralized management of the IP addresses that are used on the network. DHCP prevents IP address conflicts (where two client computers have the same IP address). The Windows systems administrator needs solid experience in configuration and administration of DHCP clients and servers in a network.

Domain: A domain is a group of computers that are part of a network and share a common directory database. A domain is administered as a unit controlled by common rules and procedures. A domain provides access to the centralized user accounts and group accounts maintained by the domain administrator. The Windows systems administrator needs to be able to manage multiple domains, domain trust relationships, and security.

Virtual Private Network (VPN): VPN is the extension of a private network that includes encapsulated, encrypted, and authenticated links across shared or public networks. VPN connections provide remote access and routed connections to private networks over the Internet. The Windows systems administrator must have experience in administering VPN for end users and also managing appropriate VPN security.

UNIX/Linux Skills Sets

The skills sets you see in a UNIX/Linux Administrator resume or in a job description requirement include the components of the operating systems that help in the administration of the users in its network, management of hardware and software components, security, and file system. Aside from being able to answer questions on how he/she configured and performed troubleshooting activities, every UNIX/Linux Administrator must be skilled with the ability to use most UNIX commands and utilities. Following are those utilities.

RESUME PHRASES   UNIX System Administrator

UNIX/Linux, Sun Solaris, Perl, C++, RCS,CVS, Postfix, QMail, Sendmail, procmail, CGI, Shell Scripting, SSH, Kerberos, DNS, NFS, SMTP, DHCP, Samba, NetBSD, FreeBSD, PGP, GPG, and X Window system.

Figure 5.4. Phrases in a UNIX System Administrator's resume.

Programming/Scripting: Scripts are used for performing administrative tasks. Administrators can write scripts that automate these tasks, making the daily and monthly tasks as simple as a click of a button. The UNIX/Linux Administrator should know how to write scripts using Perl5, Shell Scripting, and Vi Editor.

Software Configuration and Administration: There are many software available in the UNIX environment, some of which are used for Web server, directory, mail system, and domain service administration, to name a few. The list of software tools includes Apache HTTP/HTTPS

Servers, DNS, NFS, NIS/YP, POP, IMAP, IMAPS, SMTP, Postfix, QMail, Sendmail, procmail, listserv, mhonarc, PPP, FreeBSD, source code control (CVS, RCS, SCCS), and X Window System. The UNIX/ Linux administrator should be familiar with most of the listed software that run in this environment; this person should know how to use these tools to manage users, security, file systems, network resources, network access, mail systems, and optimizations.

Security: Being able to secure the UNIX operating system is an important skill that all O/S administrators must have. In UNIX the knowledge of UNIX security, firewall setup, and configuration with Juniper Netscreen and IPFilter are crucial. Local and Wide Area Network security and VPN security are also skills the administrator should have. The following are complementary security components the administrator should know: IPSEC, Encryption (PGP, GnuPG, SSL), SSH, Kerberos, Security Policy Plan, and network security auditing.

Networking: The candidate must have a practical understanding of the network protocols, such as TCP/IP, UDP, ICMP, and so on. The UNIX/Linux Administrator should know how to use simple connection commands such as Telnet (a program that lets you log in to use other computers on the network as if you were sitting in front of the other computer). In addition to protocols, the UNIX administrator should have network troubleshooting and maintenance skills, including configuring network utilities such as DHCP, SNMP, IPv6, HTTP (Hypertext Transfer Protocol), POP3 (Post Office Protocol), IMAP (Internet Message Access Protocol), SMTP (Simple Mail Transfer Protocol), DNS (Domain Name Service), LDAP(Lightweight Directory Access Protocol), and NFS (Network File System).

Mainframe Skills Sets

Mainframe system administrators perform the day-to-day tasks of maintaining business data that reside on the mainframe, as well as maintaining the system itself. Mainframe system administrators have specializations that include the database administrator (DBA) and the security administrator. Mainframe system administrators are very interested in how end-user applications are utilized and, therefore, have more interactions with end users than their counterparts in UNIX and Windows environments. Mainframe system administrators are oftentimes interfacing directly with the application programmers and end users to make sure that the administrative aspects of the applications are met.

Subsequently the system administrator role is key to the smooth operation of a mainframe system. We've identified some skills sets required for the mainframe administrator, including.

TSO/E: Time Sharing Option/Extensions (TSO/E) allows users to log on to z/OS and use a set of basic commands. It provides a log-on capability and a command prompt interface to z/OS. Most administrators work with TSO through its menu-driven interface and Interactive System Productivity Facility (ISPF). It's a given that the mainframe system administrator has the skills to use TSO/E to configure multilevel security that creates an environment that requires security label at log-on.

ISPF: Interactive System Productivity Facility provides a menu system for accessing commonly used z/OS functions. ISPF provides utilities, editor, and ISPF applications to the administrator to use in developing interactive applications. The system administrator has access to almost all z/OS system functions using the ISPF and needs to know how to manage the ISPF environment.

z/OS UNIX Shell and Utilities: The z/OS UNIX shell and utilities provide an interactive interface to z/OS, allowing administrators to write and invoke shell scripts and utilities, and also use the shell programming language. Shell scripts are a list of shell commands created with the shell programming language. Since IBM mainframe systems now include UNIX tools and utilities, the mainframe system administrator is expected to know how to use UNIX commands to perform administrative tasks in the z/OS environment.

Data Management in z/OS: Data management involves all of the system administrative tasks of data allocation, placement, monitoring, migration, backup, recall, recovery, and deletion. Storage management can be done either manually or through automated processes. The system administrator should know how to use the Data Facility-System-Managed Storage (DFSMS) utility to automate storage management for data sets.

Batch Processing and the Job Entry Subsystem (JES): Much of the work running on z/OS consists of programs called batch jobs. Job entry subsystem (JES) manages the flow of batch jobs in a z/OS system. Batch processing is used for programs that can be executed with minimal human interaction and at a scheduled time or on an as-needed basis. The system administrator should know how to use JES to manage data input and output, as well as job queues.

Workload Manager (WLM): This is a component in z/OS that manages the processing of workload in the system according to the company's business goals. This is a required skill for the mainframe system administrator.

Job Control Language (JCL): JCL tells the system what program to execute and provides a description of program inputs and outputs. The system administrator is expected to know how to use this tool to set up and administer batch jobs.

Customer Information Control System (CICS): Enables the availability of legacy system applications on the Internet. The system administrator should be able to use CICS programming commands for transactional subsystems of z/OS that run online applications.

Resource Access Control Facility (RACF): Used for securing the z/OS system, the RACF provides the basic security framework on a z/OS mainframe. The mainframe system administrator should know how to set up this framework for the purposes of identifying and authenticating users, authorizing users to access protected resources, and logging and auditing of attempted unauthorized access.

RESUME PHRASES   Mainframe System Administrator

ISPF, TSO/E, JCL, z/OS Administration, CICS, WLM Administration, System Administration using z/OS UNIX Shell and Utilities, knowledge of the main components of the IBM Mainframe zOS architecture— DFSMS, RACF, TSO, ISPF, JCL, Batch Processing and Scheduling, and JES.

Figure 5.5. Phrases in a Mainframe System Administrator's resume.

Figure 5.5 lists subsets of the skill phrases you typically find in a job description of a resume for a mainframe system administrator. And now it's easier to understand the acronyms and the skills set needed after reading the explanations above.

Conversation Between a Technical Recruiter and a System Administrator

There are some questions a technical recruiter might ask a system administrator to understand their focus. Most candidates feel that recruiters do not have much knowledge about the intricacies of their technical skills; that is why we start this recruiter-to-candidate conversation with a tone that makes the candidate feel like they can actually relate to the recruiter.

QUESTIONS

The recruiter may start by going through the preliminaries of basic recruiter and candidate greetings and afterward flow right into the interview. Please note that this exchange is based on the Windows System Administrator skills sets.

Greeting:
"Hi. My name is Helen Olive from ABC Solution. I saw your resume online and wanted to find out more about your skills sets in relation to a position I have today.... Is this okay?"

Interview:
"Help me if you will. I enjoy listening to how system administrators solve business problems. I'm going to ask you some general questions; your answers will give me a better understanding of what you do and perhaps what you enjoy the most in your job."

- *"Please describe your networking environment—the platform supported, number of users, and security configuration. Tell me about your team—how many other system administrators do you work with and how are your responsibilities divided?"*
- *"Of all the network application technologies and protocols you are familiar with, which do you work with on a daily basis? How do you use them?"*
- *"You listed Active Directory on your skills profile; please tell me how this is configured in your company. Did you inherit this configuration, or were you part of the original AD planning?"*

> - *"In your Active Directory, please tell me some of the considerations you have for designing, configuring, or managing your Active Directory environment."*

The subjects of these questions can be substituted to match any of the skills being recruited for. After this conversation, based on the answers received from the candidate, the recruiter is able to make the determination whether to move the candidate forward to the next step in their recruiting process.

Desktop versus Network Administration

How does one differentiate between a desktop systems engineer and a network systems engineer who are both certified either as a Microsoft Certified Systems Engineer (MCSE) or a Microsoft Certified Systems Administrator (MCSA)?

A network engineer or administrator is usually seen as more senior and experienced than the desktop administrator. The network engineer usually progresses to this position from desktop administration. The desktop engineer/administrator for the most part has direct communications with the end user, providing support and configuring the operating systems, applications, and network access on desktop computers. The network engineer's contact with the end user is through the desktop engineer; the network engineer designs, implements, and manages the physical and logical network infrastructure, which may include router, switch, storage, and data center configurations.

In Figures 5.6 and 5.7 are job description samples of the desktop systems and network systems administrator/engineer roles. This section will study both roles to find out the differences and similarities between desktop and network focused administrators.

SAMPLE

MCSE Desktop-System Engineer Job Description sample
Skills: MCSE, Windows 2000, Windows 2003, Active Directory, server, exchange server, MS Office 2003, TCP/IP, routing, troubleshooting, Symantec Ghost, McAfee, HP MSA SAN.

- Thorough understanding and demonstrated experience in TCP/IP, DNS, DHCP, EIGRP, OSPF, and BGP routing protocols.
- Experience with various business-class and consumer-class WAN transports, including DS3, T1, cable modem, DSL, wireless, and microwave.
- Good knowledge of various internetworking concepts, such as SNMP, PPP, HSRP, NAT, IPSec, CEF, Ether Channel, bonding, load balancing, and ATM.
- Solid knowledge in LAN, WAN, MAN, VPN, and network security technologies.

Figure 5.6. Sample job description of a Desktop Engineer.

SAMPLE

MCSE Network Engineer Job Description sample
Skills: MCSE, CCNA, network architecture, RAID, SAN technology, infrastructure design, Cisco, Enterprise class network, scripting.
- Design, implement, and maintain servers, switches, and routers.
- Implementing high availability environments, including Citrix, SQL Clustering, Active Directory, and EMC storage subsystems.
- Conducts performance tuning analysis, capacity planning, workload modeling, and forecasting.
- Experience in crafting Standard Operating Procedures (SOP) and/or Service Level Agreements (SLA).
- Good knowledge of voice and data networks.

Figure 5.7. Sample job description of a Network Engineer.

The separators are usually based on years of experience, technology environment, network storage experience, and network application implementation.

- **Years of experience**: On first look, one may immediately use this metric to separate a desktop engineer from his network engineer counterpart. But to the experienced recruiter, this is not usually so; a person may decide for any number of reasons to stay on in the role of a desktop support person even though they possess the same level of certifications and years of experience that their network engineer counterpart has. Though years of experience may be a factor that helps in the determination of whether a person is desktop or network inclined, it helps to use other metrics in conjunction with this factor.

- **Technology environment**: Just like the previous metric, this should also be used in conjunction with others to make a determination. In letting your candidate describe their environment, you as the recruiter are listening to hear their familiarity and experience in the position being recruited for. Remember that just because a person has worked in a high-profile network environment with extensive configurations of routers and network appliances, this does not necessarily mean that they were actually part of the implementation or support of this network.

- **Network storage experience**: Implementations of storage access networks (SAN) and network attached storage (NAS) are also indications of a person's alignment toward being a network engineer. Desktop administrators are more focused with end-user activities; since SAN and NAS are far removed from the end user and closer to infrastructure management, they fall into the jurisdiction of the network administrator.

- **Network application implementation**: In most cases, whenever you see reference to VPN, McAfee, and Symantec Ghost in a person's resume, this is usually an indication of the level and type of experience of the person; these are technologies used mostly on desktop environments, thus pointing to the fact that this person may be a desktop support person and not a network engineer.

What We Learned

- An operating system is software that controls the resources on the computer system, how other programs or software behave on the computer, and the overall management of a computer system's resources.
- The main capabilities of an operating system are its abilities to multitask, to provide networking between the hosting computer and other computers and peripheral devices, and to secure the contents of the hosting computer.

- There are two main types of operating systems: the desktop operating system, which may be referred to as a single-user operating system; and the network operating system, which is a multiuser operating system.

- A desktop operating system is the operating system found on client or end-user computers, such as Windows XP, Vista, and Windows 7. The network operating system is an operating system installed on a computer identified as a server in a client-server network environment; it controls the network, the resources on the network, and desktop computers attached to the same network as the server computer.

- It is important to differentiate between a desktop focused systems engineer and a network engineer, who are both certified, MCSE or MCSA. A network administrator is usually seen as more senior and experienced than a desktop administrator. The network administrator plans, configures, and implements the overall network, security, access levels, and more. The desktop administrator deals with end users and their desktop operating systems and applications, supporting and troubleshooting issues arising from end users.

SECTION THREE

Chapter 6

Software Development Life Cycle (SDLC)

In This Chapter

- SDLC in a nutshell
- Phases of Systems Development Life Cycle (SDLC)
- Job roles found in each phase
- How SDLC comes together

As a technical recruiter, you may have seen the reference to SDLC in almost every software development, quality assurance, business analyst, and project management position. It's because SDLC is the foundation for successful software development. To start and finish any project that involves other resources, there must be a plan in place that defines the role of each person, the engagement plan, progress, and hand-over process. SDLC is that plan.

With this process, a software product follows a life cycle for its creation, testing, and introduction to market. Software Development Life Cycle (SDLC) features several phases that mark the progress of systems analysis and design effort. The technical recruiter who works with candidates in software development must understand these phases, the relationships between the phases, and the job roles present in each phase.

This chapter provides an overview of all the phases of the SDLC, their deliverables, and the roles and responsibilities of each job title in a phase. The knowledge from this chapter is key for every technical recruiter looking for talent in any phase of software development. The recruiter must understand who the business analyst (BA) is, why their role is seen in most phases, and why most job requirements for the BA look for business as well as technical and documentation skills.

Reading through this chapter, a technical recruiter is able to see how the business analyst, as a result of their familiarity with all SDLC phases, can become a project manager. You can also tell the difference between a Project Manager and a Technical Project Manager and situations where one may be preferred over the other.

Figure 6.1. Software Development Life Cycle.

Looking at Figure 6.1, it may seem like the steps in the life cycle are sequential, but this is usually not the case. The steps of the sequence are meant to be adapted or used as a guideline for creating any product. Some activities in one phase may be completed in parallel with other activities of another phase. Some phases are iterative, which means that they are repeated until an acceptable system is found. The SDLC pattern used in organizations may differ from one place to another, but many of these steps are still performed for software development.

SDLC in a Nutshell

Table 6.1 shows the stages of SDLC, their deliverables, and the job roles involved in each stage.

Stage	Deliverables	Job Roles
Project Initiation & Selection	Project approval, architecture of data, network, software	Management, Data Architect, Software Architect, Enterprise Architect, Business Analyst/Product Manager
Project Planning	Business and cost analysis, business requirements gathering	Project Manager, Technical Project Manager, Business Analyst/Product Manager
Analysis	Analysis and recommendation of current and intended system, documentation	Business Analyst/Product Manager, Technical Writer
Logical Design	Functional requirement, data modeling, sources and uses of data or resources, documentation	Data Architect, Software Architect, Business Analyst/Product Manager, Technical Writer
Physical Design	Technical functional specification	Infrastructure Architect, Operations, Business Analyst/Product Manager
Implementation	Coding, testing, training, user acceptance testing, installation, configuration management, documentation	Application Developer, Database Developer, Quality Assurance, Tester, Business Analyst/Product Manager, Configuration Manager, Project Manager, System Administrator, Network Engineer, Database Administrator, Technical Writer
Maintenance	New product releases, updates, training, support, documentation	System Administrator, Network Engineer, Configuration Manager, Business Analyst/Product Manager, Technical Writer, Trainer

Table 6.1. SDLC snapshot.

Of all the deliverables in the SDLC process, the most important is the delivery of software requirements. Software requirements, as defined by Sommerville in 1997, *"are ... a specification of what should be implemented. They are descriptions of how the system should behave, or of a system property or attribute. They may [also] be a constraint on the development process of the system."* Every project needs to have a software requirement. Frederick Brooks describes the critical role of requirements process to a software project in his 1987 essay "No Silver Bullet: Essence and Accidents of Software Engineering." He states:

The hardest single part of building a software system is deciding precisely what to build. No other part of the conceptual work is as difficult as establishing the detailed technical requirements, including all the interfaces to people, to machines and to other software systems. No other part of the work so cripples the resulting systems if done wrong. No other part is more difficult to rectify later.

The three levels of software requirements according to Wiegers' 1999 book *Software Requirements* are: business requirement, user requirement, and functional requirement, of which business requirement represents the highest level of objectives to an organization. User requirement describes tasks the users of the system must be able to accomplish. These user requirements are captured in use cases, which are scenario-based descriptions of what a user should be able to do with the system. Functional requirement is software functionality that developers must build into the software product to satisfy the business requirement.

The task of creating the software requirements is often performed by the business analyst or product manager. The product manager is the owner of the product in question, creating the product or software system. In some companies, the business analyst is actually the product manager, just with another name.

As you can see from Table 6.1, the business analyst/product manager is found in all the phases. An organization may choose to have the business analyst and product manager in all the phases except the logical and physical design, where only the data architect, software architect, and infrastructure architects work to create a technical design based on the business requirements received from the business analyst and product manager.

The Business Analyst and Software Requirements

The business analyst can be found in all the phases of SDLC, sometimes as the main character, other times as just a go-to person who provides feature clarification throughout the development cycle, refining features as necessary. Right from the beginning of the project, the business analyst is the person who either created the product or, in some cases, is handed the high-level software requirement from the product manager.

In Wiegers' *Software Requirements*, several purposes of the software requirement document are stated:

- Customers and the marketing department rely on the software requirement to know what products they can expect to be delivered.
- Project managers base their plans and estimates of schedule, effort, and resources on the product description contained in the software requirement document.
- The software development team relies on the software to understand what is to be built.
- The testing team uses the product behavior descriptions to derive test plans, cases, and procedures.
- The software maintenance and support staff refer to the software requirement document to understand what each part of the software is supposed to do.
- The training team also uses the software requirement document to help them develop educational materials.

Figure 6.2 displays a sample business analyst's job description, where the responsibilities include creating business requirements and specifications, acting as a liaison between all the groups that will be affected by the new or updated product, and working with software testing teams to create test cases and test scenarios. In short, the business analyst from this job description is seen as the glue that brings all groups together and is the bridge across which all development phases must pass. As a result of the burden of being the go-to person for almost every product clarification, the BA is expected often to be a product and business know-it-all. In a later section in this chapter, we discuss the connection between the business analyst and the product manager.

SAMPLE

Overview

The business analyst has the primary responsibility to gather, analyze, validate, specify, verify, and manage the needs of the project stakeholders—clients and business users. The business analyst is part of the technology team and serves as the liaison between the business managers and the software development team. This business analyst is involved at every level of the entire software development life cycle.

Responsibilities
— Develops and maintains a thorough understanding of the needs of the group from a business and technical perspective. Works closely with development, quality assurance, systems, and customer care teams, as well as clients, to capture business requirements and see them through implementation.
— Acts as a liaison between the business user and the technical systems groups.
— Gathers, analyzes, and documents high-level business requirements. Writes detailed specifications for new or revised systems to ensure that business requirements are met by internal and/or external resources. Obtains business area sign-off.
— Analyzes existing business processes and application functionality. Translates requirements into functional designs.
— Runs queries (SQL) to analyze and test data.
— Creates test strategies and test cases to ensure quality. Performs integrated system testing and assists with user acceptance testing. Tracks defects and resolution.
— Experience translating high-level requirements into detailed business requirements and business rules.
— Develops project documentation, forms, and training manuals. Conducts training in the business process so that systems changes are understood and utilized. Updates system documentation with all system changes made.

Requirements
  - Bachelor's Degree or equivalent business experience
  - 3 + years experience in the design and development of complex business systems
  - Experience in Project Management methodologies
  - Thorough knowledge of Microsoft Office applications (Word, Excel, PowerPoint)
  - Experience with Software Development Life Cycle (SDLC)

Figure 6.2. Sample business analyst job description.

You may have noticed that the business analyst is almost always required to have some technical skills, such as T-SQL (Transact—SQL), used in querying the database. Experience in database reporting tools such as SQL Server Reporting Services (SSRS) and software testing tools also appear as requirements for the business analyst. The business analyst, as part of her responsibilities, analyzes the success of a product launch. The ability to perform this task lies in her ability to use the technical tools that provide the metrics.

Phases of SDLC

The phases of SDLC are project initiation and selection, project planning, analysis, logical and physical design, implementation, and maintenance.

Project Initiation and Selection Phase

This is the first phase of the SDLC. This is where an organization's needs are identified, analyzed, and prioritized. An organization makes a determination after the analysis of their need whether to dedicate resources to a particular project (new development or enhancement). Some criteria for selecting one project over others may depend on answers to the following questions:

- Does this project have backing from management?
- Is this the appropriate time for this project?
- Does this project improve the organization's goals?
- Are resources available?
- Is this project worthwhile in comparison to others?

Job roles in the project identification and selection phase are management, architects, and business analysts.

   o *Management*: Management analyzes and approves the system.
   o *Data, Software, and Enterprise Architects* are responsible for making sure the organization's strategic business goals are met through the use of technology. They have a wide scope of experience in business as well as technology. They are responsible for designing and creating strategies for the integration and adaptability of data, software, and network systems to the business.
   o *Business Analyst*: The Business Analyst in this phase helps with the feasibility study of the project.

Project Planning Phase

This is the second phase of SDLC, where the initial development teams comprise the system analysts, business analyst, and project managers. They develop a baseline of activities required to develop the system. In this phase, the project manager identifies all the activities and resources required to complete the project, coordinating all the activity required from the various technology groups from the user, security, design, development, and network and operations personnel. The documentation from this stage must include:

   • *Scheduling*: There should be a flexible project schedule created by each group's department, with time estimates of team members.
   • *Deliverables*: There must be a clearly defined project objective.
   • *Change Management*: The Project Manager (PM) must document a process for controlling the addition or modification of functional requirements when a project is underway.
   • *Budget*: The PM, with assistance from each department head, should produce a baseline budget estimate from each group (development, testing, and network) to ensure adherence to the project's budget.

Job roles in the project planning phase are project managers and technical project managers.

   o *Project Manager:* The role of the Project Manager is to plan, monitor, and finalize projects according to strict deadlines and within budget. This includes acquiring resources and coordinating the effort of team members and third-party contractors or consultants in order to deliver projects according to plan. The Project Manager also defines the project's objectives and oversees quality control throughout its life cycle.

o   *Technical Project Manager*: The technical project manager has all the skills and experiences of the Project Manager as well as technical abilities. This individual is technically savvy and is usually a former Senior Software Developer who got tired of coding and changed careers to manage people instead. This person understands the intricacies of working with other developers and can make better project time estimations and technical objectives definitions.

Analysis Phase

This phase of SDLC is where the needs of the system user are analyzed and documented in detail. This is where the PM and Business Analyst (BA) document what the system or software will or will not do in a requirements document. At the end of this phase, there should be a software requirements specification document.

Job roles in the analysis phase are business analysts and technical writer/ documentation analysts.

o   *Business Analyst*: The Business Analyst is a major contributor to the requirements specification deliverable. The BA must understand the business requirements of the organization in order to ensure that there is integration between business and technology. The BA has a handle on the functionalities and benefit of a software product, usually from the end user, revenue generating, and technical perspectives. The BA functions in all the SDLC phases from project initiation to implementation.

o   *Technical Writer/Documentation Analyst*: The Technical Writer develops written information about the information systems work flow and process flow. Written output includes a range of documents read by technical and nontechnical personnel in all departments. The TW documents functional specifications of a new or old system—its use, access, and capability—and coordinates and participates in training and user acceptance testing (UAT) exercises.

Design Phase

Design phase can include both the logical and physical design or can be separated depending on the individual organization. This is when the requirements are converted to a logical and physical design of the system. Data and systems modeling come into play in this stage of the SDLC. For instance, a high-level logical design of a data system may include the flow design of all the sources of business data, the areas of use, and the end result. The physical design stage includes detailed systems modeling, detailed specifications that describe all the moving and static parts of the system, and how they should work. This includes the selection of the programming language, the different software to be utilized to hardware specification, and all aspects of the system design. At the end of this phase, there should be a detailed software design document.

Job roles in the logical design phase include data architect, software architect, and technical writer.

> o *Data Architect*: In this phase the Data Architect designs the relational databases used for processing and also for data storage. This person creates the data models for the identified software applications, bearing in mind all the sources and destinations of data. These models describe the system in conceptual, logical, business, and application levels, using one of many data modeling tools like Visio, ERWin, and ER/Studio.
>
> o *Software Architect*: In this phase the Software Architect works with the Database Architect to design a system that includes all the functionalities of the application, its use, capabilities, and access.
>
> o *Technical Writer*: The Technical Writer in this phase documents the designs from the software and database architects after they have been approved.

Job roles in the physical design phase include the Infrastructure Architect and Operations Manager.

> o *Infrastructure Architect:* The Infrastructure Architect's role is to develop a high-level design plan for the overall physical

and technical IT infrastructure used for the information system or application. This includes evaluating and selecting all technologies required for the application. The goal is to design a physical infrastructure that maximizes the use of all current technology within the organization while accommodating the demand for future reconfiguration. This high-level design describes all the requirements and resources for security, backup, high-availability, storage, and network infrastructure.

o *Operations*: The IT Operations Manager works with the infrastructure architect to design the physical infrastructure requirements of the new or updated system. The infrastructure architect oftentimes works within the IT operations department.

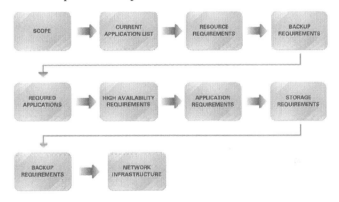

Figure 6.3. Sample development phases.

Figure 6.3 illustrates a sample infrastructure process flow of a typical system: the coding, testing, implementation, and training. In the coding stage, some of the players involved are the database developers, application developers, and user interface designers. In the testing phase, you find the configuration manager, software testers (quality assurance), and business analysts. The installation or implementation stage includes the database administrators (DBA), systems administrators, and project managers. The last phase in this sample is the training phase, which includes documentation, user acceptance testing, and then training. Remember that the roles or tasks in each phase will differ from one company to another.

Implementation

The implementation stage has two stages, which are the early and late stages. The early stage consists of coding, testing, and installation/ code propagation to a production environment. The late stage includes documentation, training, and user acceptance. Prior to the early stage, the developers would have been handed the design model and the written specification of how the system should be built and how it should work. Using this specification, the developers then begin writing code.

Between the coding, testing, and installation is a process called configuration management. This is a process of tracking different development builds/versions of the software for revision, change, and release control.

- *Coding*: The software and database developers write the code to build the system.
- *Testing*: Software testers and quality assurance analysts test the system using the test scripts and test conditions with expected results to compare outcomes to actual outcomes. When the outcome is not the same as the expected result, a defect is generated, which sets this stage back to the coding or development stage.
- *Configuration Management (CM)*: After testing has been completed, the configuration manager records and documents in a configuration management tool every code change made by developers in the testing and staging system environment.
- *Installation*: The new or updated system is then placed in the actual location where it is used by the intended workforce.

The latter part of the implementation stage includes documentation, training, and user acceptance testing (UAT).

- *Documentation*: The user guide is created by the technical writer.
- *Training*: Training is provided to the users of the system.
- *User Acceptance Testing*: This is testing performed prior to accepting transfer of ownership by the client for whom the system was designed and built. In this environment, testing is performed to ensure the system meets all the requirements specified in either the contract or the user requirements specification.

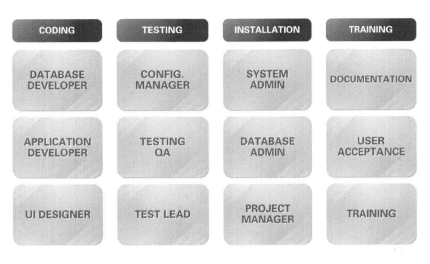

Figure 6.4. SDLC implementation phase.

Figure 6.4 displays the job roles in the implementation phase, which include the Application Developer, Database Developer, Configuration Manager, Tester/Quality Assurance, Project Manager/Business Analyst, System Administrator, Database Administrator, and Network Engineer.

- o *Application Developer*: In this phase the Application Developer starts coding based on the documented requirements.
- o *Database Developer*: In this phase the Database Developer starts coding based on the documented requirements.
- o *Configuration Managers*: The Configuration Manager in this phase moves the code written by developers from the development environment into the quality assurance environment, ready for software testers to either break or pass the software in order to validate the functions. The configuration manager uses software like SourceGear and Visual SourceSafe for version control. Each new software code written and checked in by developers is versioned and dated. It is very important for the configuration manager to know which version of code was tested and approved to be implemented in the production environment.

There are usually at least three environments, sometimes four, in most software development landscapes; these are the development, quality assurance, staging, and production environments. When code fails in the quality assurance environment, the phase goes back to development, where the developers fix the identified defect and send it back to the quality assurance environment through configuration management.

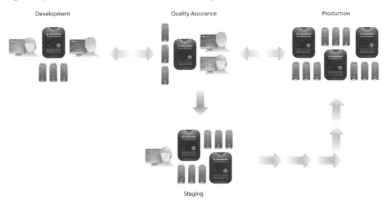

Figure 6.5. Product development landscape.

Figure 6.5 illustrates a sample product development landscape, where the development team hands off their work to quality assurance, who after testing hands off their work to the configuration manager, who hosts the product in a staging environment. A staging environment is built to be almost an exact replica of the production environment. The configuration manager, after testing to ensure the effectiveness of the new code in the staging environment, hands off to the operations team, who then propagates the code into the production environment. The dotted line from quality assurance to staging and from staging to production is there to show that the staging environment is not always available and can be bypassed.

- o   *Tester/Quality Assurance*: The Software Tester's role in this phase is to plan, design, and execute effective test cases on a software application to ensure that it functions as designed.
- o   *Project Manager/Business Analyst*: In this phase the Project Manager or Business Analyst acts as a go-to person for the quality assurance analysts and testers, answering questions arising from software functionality tests. He also facilitates meetings with all teams to discuss defects, time frame, resources, and go-live planning.
- o   *System Administrator*: This individual gets the production environment ready for code propagation. The System Administrator works with the infrastructure architect to

implement the architecture design, which includes installing required prerequisite applications and implementing the plan for security, backup, high availability, and storage. This individual gets the entire production system ready for the propagation of the code from the staging to the production environment.

o *Database Administrator*: The DBA in the implementation phase works with the system administrator in planning and implementing the go-live activities. Go-live for Web-based applications or portals requires all hands on deck: the Project Manager, to plan out the process and on-call resource list; the System Administrator, to make ready the environment and propagate the tested code to the production environment; the Database Administrator, to work with the system administrator monitoring performance of the database systems once code has been propagated; the Developer, on standby to write quick fixes if required; Testers, on standby to test any quick fixes written by the developers; and the Configuration Manager, on standby to move the tested quick fix to the staging area and prepare for the system administrator to start this whole prop process again.

o *Network Engineer*: Their role in the SDLC process is to ensure the stability and integrity of the network. For the implementation of the Web-based application or portal, the Network Engineer participates in the installation, monitoring, maintenance, support, and optimization of all network hardware, software, and communication links between the application and the users of the system.

Maintenance

The final stage of the SDLC, this phase involves the support of the working system, the enhancement of parts of the system based on users' needs in order for the continued usefulness of the system. In some ways, the maintenance phase could be said to incorporate all the other phases of SDLC. When users that purchased this system request a change in the system, the SDLC process starts all over again, including all the roles and stages, though still in the maintenance stage. Listed below are a few of the job roles in the maintenance stage.

Job roles in the maintenance phase include System Administrator, Network Engineer, Technical Writer, Trainer, and Configuration Manager.

o   *System Administrator:* Supports and troubleshoots the software implementation.
o   *Network Engineer:* Supports and optimizes the hardware, software, and communication links on the software implementation.
o   *Documentation/Trainer:* Provides end-user training and user manuals and documentation on the software best practices.
o   *Configuration Manager:* Is on standby mode, waiting for any tested code that needs to be moved from development to quality assurance environments.

How SDLC Comes Together

Everything worth doing has to be done well, right? Most things that are done right are done with a plan, especially if more than one person is involved in the game. Imagine if members of a development team are working (writing code) without regard for how the code worked with another team's code. It would be mayhem.

SDLC presents a set of guidelines and processes followed by development teams to create a software product. SDLC, when adopted well, ensures that there is a method to the madness involved in software development. Even though there are many phases in SDLC, each phase can still be broken down into other smaller processes. The number of phases adopted by each company depends entirely on its team leaders and software architects.

The combination of phases a company chooses to adopt does not matter; the important thing is that a process was adopted to manage the progress and success of the project.

Sample Software Developed with the SDLC Process

The following scenario is based on an online subscription company where 75 percent of their revenue is based on member subscription. This organization has a development team that comprises Product Managers, Technical Project Managers, Application Developers, Database Developers, User Interface Designers, Software Testers, Technical Writers, Configuration Managers, and IT Operations (Systems Administrators and Network Engineers). Each group comprises about three to eight persons in each team, including the managers or directors of each team. Business is good, and daily subscriptions are increasing. But a business must grow by at least 10 percent every year, right? So the company wants a new product or an enhancement to their product that will generate more revenue.

TIPS

In some companies, the Product Manager doubles as the Project Manager and Business Analyst. Other companies separate the tasks in two or three different persons, where the Product Manager is another name for the Business Analyst and the Project Manager is a separate person.

Stage One: Product Managers decide that the quickest way to increase revenue is from the current subscribers. Are there leaks in the system, are people gaming the system and circumventing subscriptions, are nonsubscribers getting the benefits of subscription without paying for it? The benefit of subscription is the ability to communicate with fellow subscribers and nonsubscribers. Only paid subscribers are able to communicate. So analysis starts, and ends quickly with a great find. People were in fact gaming the system.

A new product is born. There needs to be an enhancement product that checks and stops communications originating from nonsubscribers. Only subscribers can originate e-mail conversations. This analysis uncovered a significant amount of lost revenue based on this problem.

Stage Two: The analysis is packaged in a cost-benefit analysis with graphs and presented to stakeholders. Stakeholders deliberate and then initially sign off on this project based on the analysis.

Stage Three: Product Managers and/or Business Analysts and Project Managers start work performing in-depth analysis of how the product should work, creating requirement specification documents that contain use case analysis; this is the document with process flow information that describes the problems in the system and how it should be fixed. It also includes each case of a use of the system and what the expected result should be with each use. Software Architects, Data Architects, and Operations/Infrastructure Architects must be part of this stage to ensure that the requirements and the proposed fix fit within the framework of the company; and if not, they suggest how to adapt or change it.

Stage Four: After the document from stage three is complete, the Software Architects, Data Architects, Quality Assurance Manager, and Operations Managers are brought in to discuss the new product, its technicality, and the resources needed from each group. These managers then submit their resource schedule and dates, which are dependent on other project time frames.

Stage Five: The Database Developers and Application Developers start at this stage to create the functional requirements. This document describes how the problem in the requirement specification can be fixed from the database and application development level. The developers design all the moving parts of the new system and how it fits within the old one.

Stage Six: Development starts and is ready for software testing.

Stage Seven: Before testing commences, the Configuration Manager moves the code from the development environment in stage six into the testing environment. Testing can go either of two ways: 1) be successful, where there are no defects; code is then moved to the staging environment ready for production; 2) the software testers kick the code back as a result of defects, errors, or misapplied functionality. There may have been found a case where a nonsubscriber who logs into the Web site through a nonconventional means is still able to initiate an e-mail. Or the testers may find that subscribers are giving out their e-mail addresses to nonsubscribers, who can then communicate with nonsubscribers outside the system. Whatever the case, the developers go back to stage six and then seven; this iteration may go on a few times before the code is moved to staging.

Stage Eight: The Configuration Manager moves the code to the staging environment, where it is ready to be propped into production, which is ready for public use.

Stage Nine: IT Operations, comprising the systems administrators, propagates the tested code onto Web servers open to the outside world. Usually this initial propagating is performed on one server alone. This is because it will be easier to pull code out of one server if anything goes wrong during code propagation than from multiple servers.

Stage Ten: Complete? No way. The iteration can start all over from stage six again if a problem is found during or shortly after propagation. The Software Testers start testing the production implementation to confirm that the solution works the same in the real world. After the testing is complete on the one server, then the Systems Administrators propagate the code on all the Web servers.

Stage Eleven: The technical writer, who has been involved in all the stages, completes documentation on the product and stores it.

As you can see from this implementation, there was no training involved in this enhancement, yet the SDLC process was followed.

The Technical Project Manager versus the Project Manager

A project manager's main role is to plan, monitor, and finalize projects according to deadlines and within a specified budget. The main difference between the technical and nontechnical project manager is their background. The technical manager has a technical background, usually a software developer or systems administrator who has led numerous projects in the past and now has a title to go with the work she's performing. There are times when there's a need for a technical project manager (TPM) and not the usual project manager—times such as when there's a need for the project manager to understand and apply the need for using the full life cycle development in system analysis and design.

When you need a project manager who has had hands-on experience doing the same kind of work that she's now asking others to perform, the technical PM can be a better advocate for both sides—the development and the business sides. The TPM is able to communicate to the development team in a language they understand and to the business team alike. As a result of the TPM's prior hands-on experience in development projects, she may be able to make better time deliverable estimates of the work involved in a development or infrastructure project.

It is noteworthy to mention the fact that just because a job requisition requires a TPM, this does not mean that you can present anyone with technical background. When there is a need for a TPM, there is almost always a specific background experience being sought. For instance, when a company is involved with implementing a software development project, this company will seek a TPM with background in development technologies currently being used in the company. The same is true when another company is implementing an infrastructure project; the TPM required here is usually one with that background. The job and skills requirement in the requisition will usually tell you the background being sought.

Look at Table 6.2 to see the similarities and differences in the technical and nontechnical project manager.

Requirements	Technical PM	Nontechnical PM
Background	Must be software development- or infrastructure-focused	Previous experience in planning and managing large projects; does not need to have a background in technology.
Years of Experience	7+ years hands-on experience in a technical capacity	7+ years in planning and managing projects
Education	Bachelors Degree in Computer Science, Business Administration, or Engineering	Bachelors Degree in Business Administration
PMP Certification	Nice to have but not required and usually not expected	Almost always a requirement
Technical Skills	For software development: hands-on skills in SDLC, Windows/UNIX, .NET, Java, SQL Server/ Oracle, Object Oriented Development with Agile, RUP or XP, as well as project management tools	Usually SDLC and Project management tools

Table 6.2. Technical and nontechnical project manager.

Combining the Business Analyst and Project Manager

There are organizations where the business analyst and project manager are actually rolled up in one role called the product manager. I have worked in such a company. The product manager performs the combined role of the BA and PM and is generally defined as a very creative person who defines the road map of a product, creates mock-ups (prototype/model) to communicate her ideas, creates and measures a product's success metrics, and manages the project of building this product (project manager) by planning and monitoring the execution of the project to meet deadlines and budget. Figure 6.6 shows a sample of a typical product manager's job description.

SAMPLE

Overview

We're seeking an experienced, creative, high-energy self-starter to join our team. The Product Manager will own products and features and work closely with the development team, business team, partners, and other divisions to design products that make a difference.

Job Role
— Participate in the development of products road map.
— Work across functional groups and divisions to gather requirements.
— Define and write product, feature requirements, and functional specifications that articulate current and future business objectives for new products or enhancements to existing products.
— Work closely with technical staff throughout the project life cycle to ensure that interface and technical specifications and implementations meet needs of the product.
— Review milestone releases against product definition, resolving issues affecting expectations and providing direction on definition uncertainties.
— Lead cross-functional teams including developers, quality assurance, marketing, customer service, and partners to plan and launch projects on time, on budget, and on specification.

> - Ensure the quality of the product by working with quality assurance department to develop use cases, review test cases, and track feature defects.
> - Identify necessary reports, metrics, and analysis to measure the effectiveness and success of completed project.
>
> **Requirements**
> - BA/BS, preferably in technology or business.
> - Understanding of software development life cycle.
> - Strong project management skills; organized, attentive to detail, able to manage multiple time-sensitive projects.
> - Demonstrated success managing priorities and personalities in cross-functional teams.

Figure 6.6. Typical product manager job description.

You may notice that the job description in Figure 6.6, when compared to that of the business analyst in Figure 6.2, is similar. The responsibilities of the business analyst are similar to the product manager's in the way they are both required to be the liaison between all development and business teams, to define functional specifications, and to work with quality assurance to test products. They differ in two distinct areas. First, the product manager is often required to be a very creative person. Second, he is also required to manage the project, thereby acting as a project manager.

What We Learned

- To start and finish any project that involves other resources, there must be a plan in place that defines the role of each person, the engagement plan, progress, and hand-over process. SDLC (Software Development Life Cycle) is that plan.
- Software development life cycle (SDLC) features several phases that mark the progress of systems analysis and design effort. The technical recruiter who works with candidates in software development must understand these phases, the relationships between the phases, and the job roles in each phase.
- The phases of SDLC are project initiation and selection, project planning, analysis, logical and physical design, implementation, and maintenance.

o Project Initiation and Selection Phase is the first phase of the SDLC; this is where an organization's needs are identified, analyzed, and prioritized.

o Project Planning Phase is the second phase of SDLC, where the initial development team that is comprised of the system analysts, business analyst, and project managers develop a baseline of activities required to develop the system. In this phase, the project manager identifies all the activities and resources required to complete the project.

o Analysis Phase is where the needs of the system user are analyzed and documented in detail. This is where the project manager and business analyst document what the system or software will or will not do in a requirements document. At the end of this phase, there should be a software requirements specification document.

o Design Phase can include both the logical and physical design, or can be separated depending on the individual organization. This is when the requirements are converted to a logical and physical design of the system. Data and systems modeling come into play in this stage of SDLC.

o Implementation Phase is where developers start coding. Prior to this, the developers would have been handed the design model and the written specification of how the system should be built and how it should work.

o The Maintenance Phase involves the support and the enhancement of a working system.

Chapter 7

Software Development Technologies

In This Chapter

- Programming language types
- Software developments
- Development methodologies
- Development framework
- Technologies and how they are used
- Job roles in software development
- Hiring challenges and staying current with technology

Software development is the process of using a set of tools called computer language to design a program that runs on a computer to perform or automate a task. A software developer must have the ability to communicate complex ideas and logically break up problems into simple workable solutions. Another name for software development is programming; depending on the crowd, the term "developer" may mean an entirely different skills set. Sometimes this term is mistakenly attributed to land developers. This person may be very conversant with one or more computer programming languages. The software development skills set is as old as computing, and the need for the skills sets for programming will continue to be as strong as the need to have solutions to problems.

Types of Programming Languages

A programming language is the way in which a programmer instructs a computer to perform functions. There are languages created for the different types of programming, whether one is writing code that operates devices, writing operating system code, or writing code for applications that sit on top of the operating system. The two basic types of languages are low-level and high-level languages.

Low-Level Languages

The low-level languages are the ones that interface with the microprocessor on a device. They're called "low-level" not because they are not important, but because of their close proximity to the microprocessor or hardware. Microprocessors interpret instructions in terms of "off" and "on," or "0" and "1." Examples of low-level languages are the assembly and scripting languages.

Assembly Languages

Machine language is considered the native language of CPUs, but because of how tedious it is to program in ones (1) and zeros (0), almost no one writes programs in machine language. That is why there's an alternative called the *Assembly Language*. In his 2008 book *Beginning Programming for Dummies*, W. Wang notes that the purpose of Assembly Language is to make programming easier than using machine language. It replaces dozens of error-prone machine language commands with one assembly language command.

One example of assembly language is ARM—Advanced RISC Machine. ARM is an assembly language program that translates the low-level machine language into quasi English language, known as mnemonics.

Scripting Languages

Scripting language, as a result of its ability to manipulate the hardware of a computer, can also be referred to as a low-level language. Wang refers to scripting language as a system programming language. Scripting languages can be used for performing text manipulation, performing systems administration tasks, and automating tasks. Examples of scripting languages are JavaScript, Perl, and VBScript.

High-Level Languages

High-level languages are more intuitive and interpret instructions in almost understandable English. Just like in the low-level languages, the name "high–level" does not mean they are more important than the low-level counterparts; rather, the name is a result of their distance from the microprocessor.

However tedious machine language might be, it's the only language processors understand. Even after a program is written in assembly language or a high-level language such as C++, this program still needs to be translated to machine language for the processor to utilize it. This is why there are programs called *assemblers* and *compilers*. The assembler converts assembly language to machine language, while the compiler translates high-level language to machine language.

There are many high-level languages, grouped by how their programming code is structured and organized. A few of these structure groups are object-oriented, aspect-oriented, procedure-oriented, logic-oriented, constraint-oriented, and rule-oriented languages, of which we discuss object-oriented and procedure-oriented below. Wang notes that structured programming helps one organize and divide the programs into smaller and more manageable pieces.

Object-Oriented Programming: Describes how a program is broken down into various components called objects. Each object has its own data and functions (types of operations that can be performed to the data). This allows the object to stand on its own as an independent object or be related to other objects, where each object can inherit characteristics from other objects.

Procedure-Oriented Programming: In this type of implementation, programming tasks are broken down into collections of variables and functions that are separate parts of the main program.

Examples of high-level object-oriented programming languages are 1) C# (C Sharp), a .NET programming language used for creating applications; 2) Java, introduced by Sun Microsystems and used to create complete applications that run either on a single computer or distributed among servers and clients in a network; and 3) PHP, Hypertext Preprocessor, a language used for creating dynamic Web applications.

Types of Software Development

Programming is programming no matter how you look at it; the language may be different, but the technique is generally similar. Listed here are some of the popular types of software development.

Web Development

This is written code that is installed on Web platforms and interfaces with users through Web browsers like Internet Explorer and Netscape Navigator. Examples of languages used for Web development are C#, VB.NET, HTML, PHP, Perl, and Java. Companies are moving more toward converting traditional software applications to Web applications so that they can be accessed through the Internet. Examples of such conversions are from organizations like Intuit and Microsoft with their products QuickBooks and Microsoft Money, respectively. These software applications now have versions that are Web-based products and can be accessed via the Internet.

Other Web-based companies, such as Match.com and Monster.com, have harnessed the power of the Internet to create powerful products. These are just two of the popular ones. There are countless other Web-based applications from human resources, applicant tracking, and customer relationship management to vendor management applications that are subscription based and generating huge revenues for the owners. The main benefit for the Web-based software development company is the dramatically reduced cost of maintenance and support of the software. The software is now maintained at a few servers instead of a thousand different individual installations (as is the case for non-Web-based applications). Another advantage for the Web-based product is the elimination of piracy. Since the software is Web-based software, software pirates do not have copies to distribute.

Applications Development

This generally refers to software that is not Web-based. This type of software is developed for use internally by a company or individuals. Some languages used for non-Web applications are Visual Basic, C#, VB.NET, and Java. Examples of non-Web-based applications are desktop applications, time-management software, and disk copying software. To find a list of them, just look on your computer: Start > Programs (All Programs for Vista), and you will see quite a lot of them.

These days, where the programming languages used in both Web and applications developments are the same, you will find that candidates with experience in one area are easily transitioned to the other, provided that the versions remain the same. On the other hand, if a programmer is still on an older version of a program, the transition may take longer and may not be immediately attractive to a prospective employer.

Systems Development

People that develop operating systems like UNIX, Linux, and Windows are known as systems developers. On a high level, systems development is creating software that interfaces with and manages hardware. Examples of languages used for this type of development are C++ and C. The main difference between systems and applications development is that applications programs are written to provide services to users, while systems programs provide for the hardware. An example of systems programming is code that processes how a computer manages memory and allocates disks. Systems programs are the layer between applications programs and hardware. Figure 7.1 displays a simple illustration of a computer system's layers.

Figure 7.1. System layers.

Embedded Systems Development

This is the development of software for microprocessors based on noncomputer products. Examples of these noncomputer products are mobile devices, automobiles, airplanes, cameras, medical equipment, household appliances, vending machines, and toys. Languages used for embedded development are usually referred to as low-level languages; examples are Assembly Language and C/C++.

Embedded systems development is very specialized and requires low-level programming language expertise, a thorough understanding of hardware, and an in-depth knowledge of operating systems internals. Companies that create chip-based products are always in need of embedded systems developers. Figure 7.2 illustrates some examples of embedded systems devices.

Embedded System Development Devices

Figure 7.2. Embedded system devices.

Software Development Methodologies

There are many methodologies used for software development, including Agile, Rational Unified Process (RUP), Rapid Application Development (RAD), Iterative, and so on. The one chosen by the development team depends on whether a plan-driven or an agile process is preferred.

A plan-driven methodology is described by Booch and associates in their 2007 book *Object-Oriented Analysis and Design with Applications*, as one where the goal is the definition and validation of a predictable, repeatable software development process. The plan-driven methodology is characterized by following prescriptive activities, relying on well-documented processses, focusing on strategy (rather than on tactics), and managing and controlling (following detailed plans with explicit milestones and verification points within the team).

The agile methodology releases the software developers from following strict steps and allows the developers to concentrate their creative energies on the project under development. The agile process is charaterized by doing only what is necessary. It places a reliance on the knowledge of the development team, rather than on a well-documented process, focuses on tactics rather than on strategy, is iterative and incremental, and is self-organizing as opposed to predetermined (Booch and others 2007).

The technical recruiter would encounter these terms not necessarily in a candidate's resume or job description, but during a discussion centered on the development experience of a candidate and also from the hiring manager when he or she is describing their development process.

The development methodology used in an organization really depends on the knowledge of the development team and on the phase of the project. Methodologies can move from agile to plan-driven and back again to agile in one project. Because of evolution of minds and processes, there really should not be a hard and fast rule as to which methodology a developer sticks to. Each methodology has its benefits and can be mixed and matched to suit the project and team.

Usually this information will not surface unless the recruiter asks. The recruiter should ask in order to find the right candidate for the hiring organization. A candidate that is strictly focused on only one methodology may not be well-suited for an organization that mixes and matches methodologies during a development phase. See the Call Notes below for sample questions you may ask to find out more from your candidate.

CALL NOTES

"How would you describe your development process?"

"Which methodology do you use?"

"Do you find your team mixing the methodologies as it suits the project?"

"If you had the last say, which methodology would you choose?"

"Think of one particular project—what would you say were benefits of using one methodology over another for this project?"

Described next are two examples of development methodologies, Agile and Rapid Application Development.

Agile

Agile means being able to adapt on the fly; this method of software development is based on adapting, evolving, and aligning requirements and solutions during software development to suit customers' needs. The agile process is iteration based (a successive series of repeatable tasks) and thus requires face-to-face collaboration between development teams (as opposed to following strict written documents) to decide on how to follow the next iterative steps.

Rapid Application Development (RAD)

Rapid means fast, speedy, express, hurried. This method of software development requires very little upfront planning and allows for development (coding) to be done in conjunction with whatever minimal planning needs to be done. As a result, software is written very quickly. Like the agile process, it is based on iteration; but unlike agile, it involves the building of prototypes.

The business requirements and design of the system are created during the prototype construction. Prototyping helps end users and developers verify if business requirements are met; and if so, developers formalize the design in a real system. If requirements are not met in the prototype, it allows the developers to refine the prototype in iterative steps until a desired model is achieved. This methodology is used mostly in Web development.

Development Frameworks

If you have ever used a template in a word processor (e.g., Microsoft Word) or Excel to create a document, then you know how much time it can save the user. That's similar to what is found in development frameworks—application (template) generators that simplify the process of writing code for the developers.

Development frameworks started emerging in the late 1990s as tools packaged with preestablished code that helps developers jump-start on applications development. They help developers generate applications by customizing the code that's already available in the framework.

There are two different categories of frameworks: open source and commercial-for-profit. Open source refers to software where the source code is available for anyone to use, copy, and distribute free of charge. Commercial-for-profit software is the opposite; the source code is not available and can only be used and distributed with appropriate paid-for licenses. Following are three very common and the most used frameworks: .NET, PHP, and Java development frameworks.

.NET Framework

The .NET Framework is a commercial framework from Microsoft for building applications. Developers use .NET to build many applications, from Web applications, server applications, smart client applications, and embedded systems applications to database applications. Some recruiters assume that .NET is only used for creating Web-based applications, but .NET is also used for building more than Web-based applications.

Technologies and programming languages included in the framework are:

- o VB.NET
- o C#
- o Windows Presentation Foundation
- o Windows Workflow Foundation (WF)
- o ASP.NET
- o ADO.NET
- o Windows Forms

PHP Development Framework

PHP is open source (its code base is freely available), thereby encouraging developers to build frameworks of code that help other developers jump-start in developing applications quickly. There are many PHP development frameworks. Some examples of PHP frameworks available at the time of this book's writing are:

- o Symfony
- o CodeIgniter
- o CakePHP
- o Zend

Java Development Framework

J2EE is a Java platform designed for mainframe-scale computing, typically seen in large enterprises. It's used in the same way as the .NET framework.

Development Technologies and Their Uses

It's usually easier to understand what a widget is when you know what the widget does. So with this in mind, we take a look at some technologies that make up Web development, applications development, and database development, and what they are used for. We discuss a few specific development technologies below: Java, JavaScript, Java Database Connectivity (JDBC), Java Server Pages (JSP), Asynchronous JavaScript and XML (AJAX), EXtensible HyperText Markup Language (XHTML), Remoting, ColdFusion, Cascading **Style Sheets (CSS),** LAMP, Service-Oriented Architecture (SOA), and others.

Java

Java is an object-oriented programming language introduced by Sun Microsystems. Its primary use is for building software used in distributed environments (software distributed on several computers and/or servers on a network). Because of its similarity to C++ language, you may notice that a candidate with years of experience in programming who is now a Java developer almost always has C++ experience as well. It is also easier for candidates with C++ experience to transition into Java development.

Use: For creating applications that run either on single computers or distributed among servers and clients in a network.

JavaScript

Not the same as Java, JavaScript is a scripting language with its origin from Netscape. Scripting in itself is the process of writing small programs that perform small systems administrative functions.

Use: For creating very small applications that run on the Web client or server. Also used for creating pages that appear in pop-up windows.

Java Database Connectivity (JDBC)

JDBC is the Java equivalent to Open Database Connectivity (ODBC); it's included as the standard interface for Java databases. It defines how Java applications access database data.

Use: Connects Java-based programs to SQL compliant databases.

Java Server Pages (JSP)

Java Server Pages is the Java equivalent to Microsoft's Active Server Pages (ASP) and is used for dynamic Web-enabled data access and manipulation.

Use: Used for creating dynamic Web content.

Asynchronous JavaScript and XML (AJAX)

AJAX (Asynchronous JavaScript and XML) is a Web development technique used for creating interactive Web applications.

Use: It's used for creating Web pages that feel more interactive.

XHTML

The EXtensible HyperText Markup Language, or XHTML, is an HTML markup language that conforms to XML syntax.

Use: It's used during development to ensure that layout and/or presentation look the same over any platform.

Remoting

.NET Remoting is a development process that allows objects to interact with one another across application domains or computers as if they were local.

Use: Used for developing components that can communicate directly across any remote application boundary as if they were local.

ColdFusion

ColdFusion is an Internet applications development program, similar to .NET and J2EE. ColdFusion is an application server and software development framework used for the development of software and dynamic Web sites.

Use: Used for Web development (similar to .NET and J2EE).

Cascading Style Sheets (CSS)

CSS is a simple mechanism for adding style in Web documents.

Use: Used for adding fonts, colors, or spacing to Web documents

LAMP

The acronym LAMP refers to a collection of open-source software used to run dynamic Web sites or servers. The original acronym means:

o   **L**inux, referring to the operating system;
o   **A**pache, the Web server;
o   **M**ySQL, the database management system (or database server);
o   **P**HP and sometimes Perl or Python, the programming languages.

The combination of these technologies is used primarily to define a Web server infrastructure, the programming methodology for developing software, and then to establish a software distribution package.

Use: Used for Web development (similar to .NET and J2EE).

SOA (Service-Oriented Architecture)

Service-**O**riented **A**rchitecture is a collection of packaged services that allow different applications to share business processes. SOA functions where small, distinct application units can be distributed, combined together, or reused to create another business application.

Use: It allows large pieces of functionality from existing software services to be put together to form a new application.

SOAP (Simple Object Access Protocol)

For two applications to integrate, they must agree upon an explicit message structure. The challenge to integrate different applications is an age-old one. SOAP provides a solution for this. Applications that speak SOAP can easily exchange information between one another, facilitating integration.

Use: Communicates messages between disparate systems; is used to integrate heterogeneous applications.

Message Queuing (MSMQ)

Message Queuing (also known as MSMQ) is a messaging development tool for creating store-and-forward functionality for Windows-based messaging applications. MSMQ enables asynchronous communication between two different applications.

Use: For developing store-and-forward mechanism (used by message systems) between two different applications.

Visual SourceSafe

Microsoft **V**isual **S**ource**S**afe (VSS) is a source control software package for small to medium software development projects. This software manages changes to software in the development phase by incrementing the "revision number" and the name of the person that made the change.

Use: Controlling the management of multiple revisions of software during development.

API

An **A**pplication **P**rogramming **I**nterface (API) is any interface that enables one program to use facilities provided by another, whether by calling that program or by being called by it.

Use: It allows developers to produce features for software not originally included in the design.

Perl (Practical Extraction and Reporting Language)

Perl is a scripting language first used for programming with the UNIX operating system. Perl is very popular for scripting and has little or no costs.

Use: For building interactive applications.

CGI Script (Common Gateway Interface)

This is a server-side (sits on the server and not on client applications) Internet programming language program or script used to process data entered in a fill-in form.

Use: For handling form request processing.

PHP (Hypertext Preprocessor)

PHP is a programming language originally designed for producing dynamic Web pages. PHP is used mainly in server-side applications software development.

Use: Web-based applications development.

Job Roles in Software Development

We've discussed the types of software development, which include Web, applications, systems, and embedded systems development. In this section, we'll identify the job roles requirements found in Web, applications, and embedded systems development types.

Web/Applications Development

Web and applications development share similar skills sets. Recalling the definitions of Web and applications development, Web development refers to code written and is installed on Web platforms that interface with users through Web browsers like Internet Explorer and Netscape Navigator. Applications development refers to code that is not Web-based and does not interface through Web browsers, but is developed for the internal use of an organization. Both Web and applications developments use almost the same development tools and framework. For instance, the .NET development framework can be used by both the applications developer and the Web developer for software development.

Employers are looking for developers to perform development, unit test, implement, and support code. A college degree is always sought but is usually not a showstopper.

Core Requirements for .NET
- o 3+ years in ASP.NET, C#, VB.NET
- o 3+ years in XML, Web Services
- o 3+ years in HTML/CSS
- o 3+ years in MS SQL Server

Core Requirements for Open Source
- o 3+ years in PHP, MySQL
- o 3+ years in XHTML, JavaScript, CSS

Elective Requirements
- o AJAX
- o VB Script
- o Visual SourceSafe
- o Visual Studio

Embedded Systems Development

There is always a strong requirement for formalized education; this may be because the companies are looking for core engineers with electrical, electronics, or computer engineering degrees. The extent of loss incurred in design issues with device development is usually more than its Web or applications counterpart. A Web application can usually be fixed with a quick propagation of Web code, or in the case of internally (non-Web based) used application software, by downloading a patch to fix the problem. For example, when there is a design issue with your HDTV or cell phone, the cost of a recall can be very expensive. As a result, companies seek to hire highly trained individuals to work on projects with high levels of visibility, projects such as the programming involved in devices like televisions, stereo systems, and telephones. This is not to say that individuals without a degree are never viable candidates for embedded systems development.

Core Requirements
- o   BS or MS Electrical Electronics or Computer Engineering
- o   3+ years embedded design experience
- o   3+ years in C/C++ language experience

Elective Requirements
- o   Windows CE development experience
- o   ARM assembler programming experience
- o   Real-time operating systems
- o   Other experience based on the device, DSP, telephone, RFID

Hiring Challenges

The challenge in software development is much the same as in IT in general, where fast-paced change is the name of the game. As fast as the changes are coming, the developers must know how to keep the pace or be quickly left behind. New development technologies are showing up every day, whether open source or commercial. Developers everywhere have a long list of skills to stay current on.

With this challenge comes the difficulty for technical recruiters not only to keep pace with the changing technologies, but to find developers who excel at all the current development technologies. The developer is either a jack-of-all-trades or a master of one, leaving the technical recruiters and hiring managers with a vital question to answer: whether to hire a person for their specific skills or overall performance. Unless there is a glut of unemployed skilled developers, this question must be answered by the hiring manager. When recruiters do not ask or have this question answered by hiring managers, it may lead to an unsuccessful search process.

Developers in their search for a new company are always on the lookout for organizations that utilize newer technologies and are also open to research. The newer the technologies used in a company, the more appealing the job becomes to the candidate. Imagine a candidate still working with Microsoft Windows NT 4.0 Server, SQL Server 7.0, and Exchange Server 5.0. Though the software is basically similar to their more recent versions, this candidate has very outdated skills, and an organization utilizing more advanced or recent versions of these software would be unlikely to hire this candidate.

The same is true for organizations that still use older versions of software: candidates with newer skills would not touch them with a long pole unless to come in and revamp and upgrade their systems. And from consulting experience, this does not always go as planned, in that the companies sometimes backpedal on their promises to revamp their old systems. With this in mind, some candidates steer clear of companies with outdated systems, making it a hard sell for recruiters. As a result, organizations with this knowledge, who are also looking to attract the brightest of candidates, will always be on the cutting edge of technology.

Staying Current

As people turn to easier ways to getting things done, developers and the companies that hire them will always be searching for and creating new ways, methodologies, technologies, and paradigms that make the process of development easier and faster.

With this in mind, there will always be things out there that the average technical recruiter has never heard of or seen. The following section describes some of the ways to stay current.

Google
When you stumble upon a term either in a job description or resume of which you know nothing, the trick is to know where to find it and

read about it. One word—Google. One way to easily find the definition of a word without having to read a whole page is to go to Google and type define:"word in question." An example is seen in Figure 7.3, where the definition of OOP (Object-Oriented Programming) is sought by typing in the Google search box the exact term without the quotes: "Define:OOP." The results of this search will list short descriptions of the term.

Figure 7.3. Google definition search.

Free Magazine Subscriptions
The eWeek technology magazine is one of the free technology magazines that you can subscribe to at no cost. You can go to the Web site of the publisher, www.ziffdavisenterprise.com, to learn how to subscribe.

Outlook E-mail RSS
Really Simple Syndication (RSS) is a way for content providers to make content available to subscribers. You can add an RSS feed for a particular technology or topic as a subscription in Microsoft Outlook (2007) or Internet Explorer. The benefit of RSS is that it aggregates all content from multiple sources into one place so you don't have to go to numerous Web sites to find the information you want.

If you already know the Web address of an RSS feed, you can enter the address into Microsoft Outlook software by taking the few steps outlined in the following section. You can also visit an RSS feed directory, such as rssfeeddirectory.org or microsoft.com/rss/ to search for a list of topics to subscribe to.

If, for example, you are looking to find more information on "SAP Customer Relationship Management CRM," the link is http://www. crmexpertonline.com. Search the page for the RSS icon. When found, click on the RSS feed link, which displays a page that allows you to subscribe to the content on that page. You can subscribe to this content either using your browser or using Microsoft Outlook.

Internet Explorer: Just click on the link that says "subscribe to feed." This will subscribe you to this content. You can open and close your subscriptions by clicking on the favorites button in your Internet Explorer program.

Outlook: Copy the URL of the RSS feed page. It's http://www. crmexpertonline.com/rss/news.xml in this case. Open your Microsoft Outlook program. Click on "Tools," then "Account Settings," then "RSS Feed Tab," then click on the "New" button. Paste the RSS feed URL into the section provided. Select the options that suit you or accept the default option for this feed. The RSS feed will be highlighted with the number of unread content in your mailbox.

TIPS

Please note that the Internet has inherent security risks, so be careful of giving any personal information. RSS feeds do not require that you provide your name, e-mail address, or other personal information.

What We Learned

- The two basic types of programming languages are low-level and high-level languages. Examples of low-level languages are machine language, assembly languages, and scripting languages.
- The low-level languages are called so because of their proximity to the processor. Similarly, high-level languages are called so because they are further away from the processor. Examples of high-level languages are Java and VB.Net.
- The types of software development are categorized by **Web development, applications development, systems development, and embedded systems development.**
- Software development methodology is described as the processes used in creating software. The methodologies can either be plan-driven or agile and include Agile, Rational Unified Process (RUP), Rapid Application Development (RAD), and Iterative. The one chosen by the development team depends on the team and the phase of the project in development.

- Development frameworks are like templates that developers use to jump-start their development. They include pre-established code that eliminates mundane tasks that would otherwise need to be coded by the developer from the start. There are open source frameworks as well as commercial grade ones. .NET framework and the PHP development framework are common examples.
- Staying current is a challenge for all parties: the developers, hiring organizations, and recruiters. As the challenge deepens for the developers and their organizations, the recruiters must also seek ways to stay within the relevant technology corridor.

Chapter 8

Software Testing

In This Chapter

- Software testing versus quality assurance
- The software tester's role
- Types of testing
- Skills sets for the tester
- Study of a software tester's job description
- Reviewing candidates for software testing

Imagine how it would feel entering all your information into a Web form on a Web site, hitting the submit button, and then seeing an error message requiring you to reenter all your information from the start—frustrating to say the least. This is how many users feel every day using inadequately tested software or products. When applications, Web sites, and electronic products are inappropriately tested, the company's integrity is at stake; this is one of the reasons why testing is very important. It is the same reason companies dedicate a lot of time, energy, and resources to ensure the quality of their products.

In this chapter, software testing will be elaborated on in the context of a job role, as well as a process. Software testing is also compared to quality assurance to find out the differences between them. We will also look at the reason testers prefer being referred to as Quality Assurance Analysts instead of as Software Testers. Other sections in the chapter will review the role and skills sets of the software tester.

It's important for technical recruiters to understand software testing, its challenges, and its recruiting outlook in the coming years. If software development skills in .NET, Java, and SQL are still the most sought-after skills, then it makes sense that the testing of applications developed with these skills sets would be equally as important.

In the words of Scott Gaudet, a technical recruiter with Halo Group, "Software testing would always have a strong presence onshore." His reasoning is that no matter how much of software development is sent offshore, the testing of the software to ensure it meets quality and user acceptance will be performed onshore. As a result, the need for onshore software testers will remain high.

What Is Software Testing?

Software testing is a process of verifying and validating that a software application works according to documented business specifications and technical requirements and is without defects, bugs, variances, or errors. Software bugs are inconsistencies or discrepancies causing software to act in a way that was not included in the specifications or not act in the same way as documented in the specifications.

What Does a Software Tester Do?

In R. Patton's 2006 book *Software Testing*, he states that the goal of a software tester is to find bugs, find them as early as possible, and make sure they get fixed. He lists the traits of a software tester as:

- o Explorers: Not afraid to venture into the unknown.
- o Troubleshooters: Good at figuring out why something does not work.
- o Relentless: Trying until they find a bug that's hard to recreate.
- o Mellowed perfectionists: They strive for perfection but know when to stop.
- o Tactful and diplomatic: As bearers of bad news, they know how to tactfully inform developers of bugs.
- o Persuasive: Good at demonstrating why a bug needs to be fixed.
- o Knowledgeable of software programming: Knowledge in programming languages gives the tester another testing

dimension—an understanding of how software is written and, therefore, how to test it.

Software Testing versus Quality Assurance

Quality Assurance is generally defined as a process of consistently setting and carrying out standards to monitor and improve overall performance of a project, while software testing is seen as a segment of quality assurance that deals with checking a software program to ensure that it meets its intended purpose. In essence, quality assurance is a more holistic way of dealing with an overall objective of abiding by a set of defined quality standards, while software testing checks for defects in a product. The majority of the software testers I know (myself included when I worked as one at Match.com) would like to see themselves as quality assurance analysts, though 95 percent of the job they perform on a day-to-day basis is actually software testing.

No matter how many people are bent on differentiating software testing and quality assurance, the technical recruiter should steer clear of this puddle unless it involves or generates higher pay for your candidates. If a candidate prefers to be called a Quality Assurance Analyst, then refer to this person as such; the same should be true for a Software Tester.

There are times when the employers use one title or the other depending on a number of reasons, ranging from visibility of the job on the job board to how much they are willing to pay for the more respectable-sounding title. There was an instance at a company I once worked at where a title "Report Writer" was changed to "SQL Server Data Analyst" to attract more candidates, and it worked. The content of the job description was the same; the only change was the title, and the resumes started coming in.

When you think about the titles Software Tester or Quality Assurance Analyst, hmmm, which one would a candidate choose to have on their business card? I would daresay the Quality Assurance Analyst title wins the day and attracts more remuneration.

The Software Tester's Role

Although the difference can sometimes just be in the title, there are also some differences in the tasks. Software testing is the process of testing software to ensure that it's working according to specifications. The tester validates and verifies that a software application or process meets the specific objectives of its intended purpose. The software tester must be very knowledgeable about the business and technical requirements of a product in order to test it appropriately. Some of the tools/skills the tester must have may depend on the particular software environment, but the basic skills sets are the same: writing test plans, finding important defects, and patience with working with developers.

The software tester is an inquisitive person, finds the one bad apple in the midst of two thousand others, and questions everything because that's the only way to find answers. The software tester should be detail-oriented.

The software tester works for a lot of people in the development team, some of which are:

- Business Analysts (BA), who write product specifications and their use cases. The software tester liaises with the BA to ensure that they understand the product functionalities and can therefore devise appropriate test plans. The BA sometimes acts as a go-between for the tester and programmer when discrepancies occur in how functionalities are perceived to work.
- Project Managers (PM) want to know as soon as possible if the project is being delayed as a result of a defect. The tester works with the PM to ensure they understand the time frame of the project, and then works within this time frame in creating test plans, executing tests, and reporting on defects.
- Developers or programmers also want to know as soon as a defect or bug is discovered in a system. The tester will, depending on the test reporting process in a company, pass or fail a test and direct the failed test to the developer, who fixes the problem. The process starts again, until the project has passed most tests and is deemed to be not only bug-free but to deliver on its intended promise.

Software Testing Team Members

Though the software tester interfaces with developers, business analysts, and project managers on a daily basis, the software testing core team consists of other software testers, the test manager or lead, and the configuration manager. As a team, their job is to ensure that software testing as a process is performed well. Figure 8.1 shows the members of the software testing team.

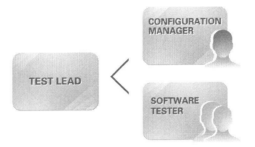

Figure 8.1. Other software testing team members.

Test Manager: This person handles resource planning, resource utilization, and work forecast. The lead works with the database administrators and systems administrators in setting up the test environment and the performing data refresh. The lead is often the person that presents the status reports to the project managers and other stakeholders. They communicate and escalate any testing concerns from team members to appropriate leads.

Configuration Manager (CM): The CM manages and controls all changes to code used in the different environments (development, testing, and production) during the software development process. He performs regular builds (labels a collection of code) and release management in these environments. The CM uses one of several version control software, such as Visual SourceSafe, ClearCase, or Vault, to manage the check-in and checkout of code.

Types of Testing

In this section we review software testing types, which are different from the testing methods. There are two methods of testing: manual and automated testing. A software tester either manually tests with their hands and eyes or writes code to perform the test more quickly.

Manual Testing: This is a method of testing that involves the software tester carrying out a step-by-step systematic process of checking for defects. To perform manual testing, the tester has to follow a written plan referred to as the test plan. Manual testing can be done with the aid of software applications. The process for conducting a manual test includes:

o   Writing a test plan, the equivalent of the project plan for the project manager. It includes the purpose and scope of the test; features to be tested; the strategy, resources, and testing methods to be deployed; the test tools; pass and fail criteria; the deliverables; and the start and end dates.
o   Writing detailed test cases that illustrate step-by-step actions to be taken by the tester and also the expected results.
o   Executing the steps in the test cases.
o   Documenting the test report.

Automated Testing: This is a method of testing where a software tool actually does the testing instead of a person. There are cases when this method of testing is better than the manual test. Some reasons for utilizing automated tests are:

o   The ability to run a large number of functional tests at any time of day and quickly.
o   To ensure thoroughness and accuracy when tests are run repeatedly over time.
o   Freeing up software testers'from repetitive testing so they can concentrate on more creative or strategic quality initiatives.

Types of software testing are classified by the purpose of the test. The different purposes form the basis for the types. For instance, if the purpose is to test the performance of a given application, then the type of test is referred to as a performance test. Other software testing types described below include black-box testing, white-box testing, gray-box testing, functional testing, regression testing, smoke testing, and stress testing.

Black-Box Testing: This type of testing approach is called black box because the tester does not have access to the inner workings of the software; he/she only tests how the software functions. For example, in testing a member registration Web form, the black-box tester enters first and last names, address, and contact information values into a Web form in different orders and expects a certain result. Figure 8.2 displays a Web form that is usually tested using black-box testing.

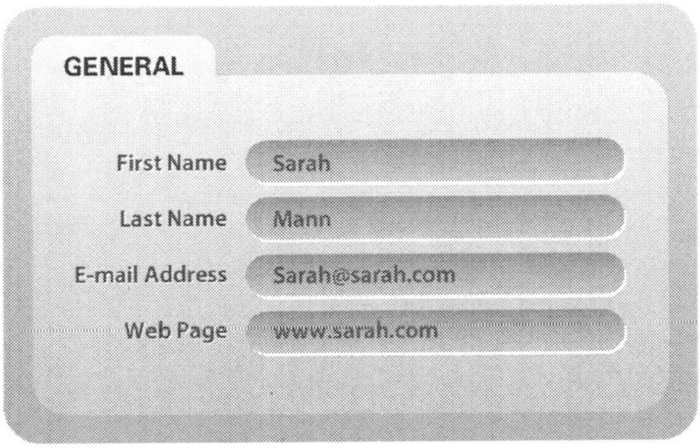

Figure 8.2. Black-box testing a Web form.

White-Box Testing: This requires some programming or software development skills. In this type of testing approach, the tester knows about the inner working of the code and can tweak the code to generate another type of result. This is the type of testing usually performed by software testers who were software programmers in previous careers.

Gray-Box Testing: This is a hybrid of both black- and white-box testing. A testing approach is referred to as gray box when both the black- and white-box testing approaches are used.

Functional Testing: Functional testing can sometimes be referred to as black-box testing. This is testing the functions of a program or application to ensure it works according to the specifications. Functional tests are carried out with the end user in mind, so this type of test confirms that the applications would perform the way users would expect.

Performance Testing: There are times when Web-based software applications accept hundreds of thousands of hits simultaneously. During the development and testing of this software application, it may not be possible to manually simulate the type of load that may occur on this program in order to experience the type of bottleneck or problem that may exist in the software with such loads. Performance testing is the process of automating the simulation of increased load and stress on a system in order to find and eliminate bottlenecks on the systems and also to establish baselines for future testing—baselines that will answer questions like how many users an application can support simultaneously with optimal performance.

Regression Testing: With new features added to applications all the time, software testers must ensure that the introduction of new features does not break the working conditions of the old ones. Regression testing is the process of retesting changes to a software application to ensure that old functionality still works with the introduction of new changes.

Smoke Testing: This is a quick test performed on a piece of software to verify that the major functionalities of the software are in working condition. The major parts for a simple Web-based application are to verify that new users are able to register and that buttons actually perform tasks. This is by no means an exhaustive test. The term, derived from the hardware industry, suggests that after a hardware component was changed or repaired, the equipment was declared as *passed* if there was no smoke after it was powered up.

Stress Testing: This is the process of testing a system to evaluate the factors that can break the system, the conditions under which a system fails, and how the system fails. There are many creative ways to fail a system, including running processes that hug system resources, thereby depleting the resources for other computer operations, and purposely stopping a required computer service. The objective of the stress test is to find out how a system responds to failure. The ability of the system to recover when the failure element is removed is the desired result of this type of test.

Stages of Software Testing

Software testing has stages that define the various activities that are performed to start and complete a software testing cycle. These activities fall into the test planning, test analysis, test design, and verification categories.

Test Planning: Software testing may seem like an easy task, but in reality it is not. There are so many moving parts involved in testing that require the availability of a plan of action. This action plan can include various moving parts, such as the types of testing (functionality, performance, or a combination of many testing types), the scope of software to be tested (identifies individual features or all features to be tested), the resources available to perform the tests, and the test schedule and budget. Though the software testing manager and the project manager are principally responsible for formulating this plan, any experienced software tester is also able to produce this plan in association with the project manager. The project manager's involvement is in ensuring the budget and schedule are aligned with the overall project plan. This plan is usually written following the sign-offs of the product specifications and business requirements documents, which occur before developers begin coding.

Test Analysis: This stage occurs before the beginning of the coding stage in the Software Development Life Cycle process (SDLC). This is when decisions are made in regard to the mechanism (manual or automated) and types of testing required for each stage of the SDLC. Test cases that describe the items to be tested and the steps followed to verify that the software works, according to business requirements and specifications, are created in this stage. The test cases are written by the software testers involved in performing the actual tests.

Test Design: This stage is basically a revision and review stage where documents from the planning and analysis stages are revised, reviewed, and signed off by the business analysts, project managers, and testing managers. This stage also includes preparing all test data and scripts in readiness for executing the tests.

Verification: Testing starts in this stage, automated and/or manual for each type of testing identified for the SDLC stage. From functionality, performance, and stress to regression testing, the process continues. Defects or bugs are identified and reported to be fixed.

Testing Skills Sets

Software testing can be both boring and exhilarating, giving the tester a reasonable amount of adrenaline when an important defect is found. Here are some very basic skills sets a software tester must possess.

o   Must be able to describe the testing process. No matter how junior a tester is to the testing environment, understanding and describing a testing process should be expected.

o   Must understand Software Development Life Cycle (SDLC) and where testing falls within the process.

o   Should be able to describe the difference between black-box, white-box, and gray-box testing.

o   Experience with at least one software testing tool.

o   Should have a good technical background. A person cannot really test software if they do not have the appropriate technical background.

o   Experience with at least two to three types of testing, including automated, regression, functionality, and performance testing.

o   Some level of experience writing test plans and test cases.

SAMPLE

SOFTWARE TESTER Profile

- Six years experience in software testing, software engineering, SDLC on multiple platforms and industries.
- Extensive experience doing both manual and automated testing on E-business/E-commerce, desktop, and client-server applications.
- Experience in testing Java Enterprise Edition (J2EE), VB.NET, C#, ASP.NET based applications on Linux/UNIX (for J2EE) and Windows platforms.
- Extensive experience in performing data validation and manipulation using T-SQL on SQL Server and PL/SQL and SQL*Plus on Oracle.
- Experience developing test plans and test cases for the Functional, Security, Integration, Regression, Load, Performance, and Usability (UAT) testing.
- Experienced in creating test automation harnesses for regression testing.

TECHNICAL SKILLS

- Test Tools: WinRunner, QTP, LoadRunner, Test Director, and Quality Center 9.0.
- Databases: Oracle 9i, SQL*PLUS, PL/SQL, SQL Server 2000/2005, T-SQL, SSRS,MS Access.

- Operating Systems: Windows 2000/2003 Server, UNIX/Linux.
- Technologies: .NET(C#, VB.NET), J2EE, Web Services, Remoting, C++, VB Script, JavaScript.
- Methodologies: Waterfall, Extreme Programming, and Agile.

PROFESSIONAL EXPRERIENCE
- Ensured that overall manual and automated testing ratio was maintained at 50:50.
- Created test cases based on application functionalities.
- Responsible for preparing and presenting weekly progress report on testing activities within the team.
- Performed Black-Box/Regression and White-Box testing on online subscription applications that included Web services, API's and Remoting, and Message Queuing.
- Worked with developers to resolve identified defects.
- Verified data integrity using T-SQL queries, and validated test results with the expected results.
- Used Quick Test Professional (QTP) for regression testing of new builds.
- Developed UAT test scripts for new functionalities.

Figure 8.3. Sample software tester resume.

Looking at Figure 8.3, you can see that the software skills sets found in a software tester can sometimes be similar to those of a programmer on paper. The differences lie in their level of experience and how the knowledge is utilized. Most testers are like consultants, who have experience and knowledge in a wide range of environments and technologies but do not have the depth to actually write code or do development. These days the trend is shifting just a bit, where you may find a few software testers who were formerly software developers. Their reasons for transitioning to testing may range from burnout to sheer preference. The developer-turned-tester may excel in white- and gray-box testing, where they can leverage their development skills.

Study of a Software Tester's Job Description

When you study any job description, there are always key skills that you pay close attention to. As you identify them, mark or underline these, as they will form the must-haves for the job role. Following the guidelines in the Anatomy of a Technical Job Requisition section found in Chapter One of this book, you may want to find out more about this job description from the hiring manager.

Depending on your experience in recruiting for a particular job role, reviewing a job description for a position you've recruited for several times before may become an automatic process for you. This is because you now know all the requirements by heart, especially if the position is for an established client or a chosen industry vertical, such as legal, medical, hospitality, or government.

Looking at the software tester job description in Figure 8.4, you will notice that the must-haves have been identified with the underline format; these are the points that will be further analyzed. When analyzing a job description, the two questions you ask yourself are: *"Why does the hiring manager want this skill?"* and *"How will this skill help the candidate perform better at this job?"*

Software Tester Job Description

The software tester will test and verify software products before they launch.

SAMPLE

Responsibilities

1. <u>Work closely with development</u>, project management, marketing, and other groups.
2. Provide scopes, <u>test plan</u>, and <u>test cases</u> to the QA Manager and all QA team members involved in the project.
3. <u>Present the test plans</u> and test cases to the QA team.
4. Ensure usability and customer experience is covered in all test cases and test plans.
5. Participate in all <u>code reviews</u> pertaining to the project.
6. <u>Justify the business impact</u> for each change or bug found.

> 7. Regression/stress test the applications with any regression testing tools.
>
> **Requirements**
> - 3+ years software testing experience
> - 2+ years experience in T-SQL programming
> - 2+ years experience in testing C#, VB.NET applications
> - 2+ years experience in automated testing

Figure 8.4 Sample job description for a software tester.

Responsibilities and Requirements Analysis

Let's begin with analyzing the responsibilities and requirements identified in the Figure 8.4 sample job description for a software tester. After the analysis, you will be able to communicate better with the candidate and be able to identify at the outset when a candidate does (not) meet the needs. The candidate, in turn, will respect your grasp of your client's technology environment and will likely open up more to you because he/she feels you are on similar wavelengths.

Work with developers: Because the tester's job is to find errors (whether bugs or defects) made by developers, the inherent relationship between these two groups is usually just a little contentious. Though each group makes a great effort to mask this contention, it's still a little difficult for some developers when informed (maybe more than once) that their code was bug-ful. With this in mind, there must be a peer relationship between the testers and developers where the tester is not afraid to voice his opinions and communicate on product requirements and user expectations. The tester must be confident in his ability and not see himself as the bug-finder but as a key member of the development team, whose full participation is required and expected.

Test plans/test cases: The tester must be able to write test plans and test cases to support the product specifications. Companies usually have templates from which all test plans and cases must be written. The test cases documentation must be very comprehensive to cover every use case scenario of the product being tested. The tester must also be able to present these documents to the team for peer review.

Code reviews: The audience for code reviews used to only be developers, but now with the software testing process starting from the very beginning of the product, testers are encouraged and required to participate in the review of developers' code. In this review, developers reveal the flow and reasoning behind their code for the review of their peers. The software tester is not required or expected to critique the code, but to listen and understand the inner working of the software development for white-box testing.

Justify business impact of defects: Pointing out another person's mistakes is very easy and comes without difficulty to most human beings. One lesson software testers know far too well is to be able to find the important defects at the onset of testing. The important bugs might be subjective based on the tester (may not be as important to one tester as to another), so in order to eliminate the subjectivity, the tester must be able to write a justification of why this defect must be fixed and the impact it has on the overall product if left unfixed.

T-SQL Programming experience: This experience is required for white-box testing of the database systems used for software applications.

Reviewing a Software Tester

Once a technical recruiter understands software testing as a whole, it becomes easier to go through the qualification process of ensuring that a particular candidate is better suited to a certain job. Software testing is one of those straightforward positions to recruit for.

The skills sets are mostly tools-based; this means that when the software tester is very knowledgeable in a software testing tool, the other skills sets will be easier to acquire if they are not already there. With a great percentage of software becoming Web-based, there is a bigger demand for software testers with Web testing experience than the traditional non-Web-based software.

For instance, the software tester with six years experience in the telecommunications hardware industry may not be the right candidate for a Web applications company. Their differences can be found in several ways, such as during the review of their resumes and in conversation with candidates to find out their experience in a particular mode and pace of testing. Table 8.1 displays key differences between a tester with telecoms experience versus one with Web applications experience.

Differentiators	Telecommunications Company	Web Applications Company
Testing Cycles	Once in month or two months	Twice a week
Test Without Test Plans	Must have a traditional documented test plan and test cases that have been signed-off by stakeholders before testing commences	Tester in this environment must be able to perform tests without a test plan.
Release Cycles	Once a month/quarter	Once or twice a week
Pace	Slow and steady	Very fast-paced, though sometimes there's not much to do
Average Hours	40 hours per week	45–50 hours per week
Software	Operating system-based software tools, more specialized tools	.NET, Java, Windows , UNIX/Linux, readily available Web application tools

Table 8.1. Differentiators between software testers with telecoms experience versus Web applications experience.

When a software tester's resume includes the fact that there were software releases or testing cycles once or twice per week, that's a very clear indication that the candidate worked for a fast-paced company. This indication will help the recruiter in identifying the environment better suited for the candidate and the hiring company alike.

Questions for the Candidate

There are many software testing interview questions one can ask a candidate. Here are a few simple questions that will give the recruiter a feeling for the technical as well as the overall fit of the software tester.

QUESTIONS

- *"Explain your typical software testing environment."*
  - o   The answers here should include how many testers, how many other software programmers, SDLC, white-box/black-box testing, and automated/manual testing.
- *"In a typical month, how many release/testing cycles did your last company have on a weekly basis?"*
  - o   The answers will tell you the pace of the development cycle.

- o If the answer to the above question is from one per week to two per week, then there is a high possibility that the tester did not have the time to write test plans or test cases for each of the tests. The follow-up question would then be … you guessed it

- *"How often did you write test plans/test cases for the tests you ran?"*

- *"Of all the testing you performed at this company, what is the ratio between the automated versus manual testing or what percentage was manual and what was automated?"*

  - o Because testers are not programmers, some testers fail to acknowledge any automation projects performed in the past in fear of being passed off as an automated tester. Automation skill is a great skill to have as a tester, so as a recruiter, you want to ensure that you capture this experience (no matter how small).

- *"How much experience do you have with back-end testing, especially with T-SQL?"*

  - o Figure 8.5 is a set of T-SQL sample questions to ask your candidate to ensure that they have basic experience with T-SQL. Here are the answers:
    - ▪ Question One: five columns and six rows
    - ▪ Question Two: EID. Reason is that this column qualifies as a unique column and therefore is the column that identifies the row
    - ▪ Question Three: SELECT * FROM Employee, or SELECT EID, First, Last, City, Position FROM Employee
    - ▪ Question Four: UPDATE Employee SET City = 'New York'

Review the table and answer the following questions.

Table name: Employee

EID	First	Last	City	Position
1001	Kelli	Clark	New York	Manager
1002	Sophie	Herring	New York	Accountant
1003	John	Henry	Dallas	Manager
1004	Vin	Redding	Austin	Customer Service Rep
1005	James	Wesley	Cleveland	System Admin
1007	Jose	Cruz	New York	Manager

1. How many columns and rows does this table have?
2. In the table above named Employee, which column would be the *primary key* and why?
3. Write a query to get all of the table's records.
4. Write a query to update the table so that all employees live in the same city—New York.

Figure 8.5. Sample prescreen questions for the
software tester involved in data validation.

What We Learned

- Software testing is a process of verifying and validating that a software application works according to documented business specifications and technical requirements and is without defects, bugs, variances, or errors.
- Software bugs are inconsistencies or discrepancies in software acting in a way that was not included in the specifications, not acting in the same way as documented in the specifications, or plainly not working right.
- The goal of the software tester is to find bugs, find them as early as possible, and make sure they get fixed. The software tester's role is to validate and verify that a software application or process meets the specific objectives of its intended purpose. The software tester must be very knowledgeable about the business and technical requirements of a product in order to test it appropriately. Some of the tools/skills the tester must have may depend on the particular software environment, but the basic

skills sets are the same: writing test plans, finding important defects, and patience when working with developers.

- Types of software testing are classified by the purpose of the test. Software testing types include black-box testing, white-box testing, gray-box testing, stress testing, regression testing, and functional testing.

- The two methods of testing are manual and automated testing. A software tester either manually tests with their hands and eyes or writes code to perform the test automatically.

- Software testing has stages that define the various activities that are performed to start and complete a software testing cycle. These activities fall into the test planning, test analysis, test design, and verification categories.

SECTION FOUR

Chapter 9

Database Technologies

In This Chapter

- Characteristics of database applications
- Database languages
- Database objects
- Database terms
- Database solutions

It's said that information is power; well, building a database is the beginning of this power achievement. Take, for instance, the software application that recruiters work with every day, the *applicant tracking system*. This is a very good example of a simple database application, where candidates enter data like first name, last name, phone number, e-mail, location, skills set, and so forth. The recruiter uses this information to make determinations as to why, who, and when to call a candidate. These days most companies with a Web presence almost always have a database behind the scenes. They collect data such as first name, last name, e-mail address, zip code, and so on. How is the data stored, for how long, and how is it retrieved and manipulated to give decision-making information? These questions are all related and are answered here.

This chapter discusses databases and the many aspects of database technologies used in business intelligence, reporting, database development, administration, data warehouse, and data mining. Here we look at two major database software manufacturers and how their software compares to each other. Read further to find out how database technologies are utilized today.

Characteristics of Database Applications

Database applications fall into two main categories, and the characteristics of these application types have a strong effect on how they are designed and implemented. The two are *Online Transaction Processing* (OLTP) and *Online Analytical Processing* (OLAP), which can also be referred to as a Decision Support system.

Online Transaction Processing: OLTP database applications are great for managing changing data. A typical OLTP application has many users who perform transactions at the same time in which data is changed in real time. Common examples of these types of databases are airline ticketing systems and banking transaction systems. The primary consideration in designing these kinds of database applications is atomicity.

Atomicity is a relational database management system (RDBMS) concept that guarantees that a transaction is either completed in full or not completed at all. Imagine starting a withdrawal transaction at a local ATM, and just before your cash comes out, there's a power failure. I imagine you would want this transaction to fail—that is, roll back to the state it was in before you started this transaction, as if you never attempted it in the first place. This is atomicity, the concept of all or nothing transaction processing.

Online Analytical Processing—Decision Support: Decision-support database applications are best for running queries that do not change data. Common examples of these types of database applications are found in business intelligence applications. In a business intelligence application, a company's senior management can run reports (querying the data) that summarize its sales data by date, region, product, store, and salesperson. This enables management to determine trends in sales quickly and make business decisions. The primary consideration in designing these kinds of database applications is indexing.

Indexing, in its simplest terms, is the process of classifying data in order to find information quickly. An example of this is what you find when you use book indexes to locate text in a book. OLAP applications usually contain huge repositories of historical data, which can run into terabytes of data. As a result of the sheer size of data in OLAP systems, it's imperative that information is retrieved as quickly as possible (usually on the same day) when a query is executed. Complex indexing is employed in order to accomplish faster access to query results, which would otherwise take several hours to retrieve.

Database Languages

Structured Query Language, SQL (pronounced SEQUEL), is a standard language for accessing and manipulating database systems. SQL was adopted as a standard by the American National Standards Institute (ANSI) in 1986. There are three main language categories of SQL: data manipulation language (DML), data definition language (DDL), and data control language (DCL).

Data Manipulation Language (DML) is the category of SQL language used to add, update, and delete data in a database. Some DML language constructs are INSERT, UPDATE, and DELETE.

The Data Definition Language (DDL) is used in the management of the table structure used to create and modify database objects. Some DDL language constructs are CREATE, ALTER, and DROP statements.

The Data Control Language (DCL) is used to control how users access data. Some DCL language constructs are GRANT, which allows users access to database objects, and REVOKE, which is used to remove a grant that was previously given to a user.

Database Objects

Database objects are the tangible components that make up a database. The database developer (sometimes called database engineer, DBE) creates them, and the database administrator (DBA) maintains and supports them. Some of the objects that make up the database are tables, stored procedures, views, functions, and triggers. When you look at a job description for the DBE or DBA (see Chapter Ten), you will note that knowledge and good experience in the manipulation and maintenance of these objects are important skills. It's more or less like a carpenter, who needs to have good experience handling hammers and nails.

Tables: These are database objects that contain rows and columns. These rows and columns store the attributes of an item. Take, for instance, an item named *customer*. Customer is the table name, and it stores all the attributes of customers, such as company name, contact name, address, phone number, and e-mail address. An example of a database table is shown in Table 9.1.

CustomerID	FirstName	LastName	CompanyName	Telephone
1001	Derek	Haynes	Venair	214-989-0098
1002	Jonna	Cruz	Post	888-909-9098
1003	Christine	Peters	Kumana	512-074-6789
1004	John	Woods	Pascal	713-454-4004

Table 9.1. Sample table.

Stored Procedures: Sometimes called *Procs*, these are the most-used programmatic objects in a database. They are a collection of SQL (see description above) statements saved and executed automatically in the database. Stored procedures can be used to validate data, control database access, return database results (results of a SELECT statement), and also to hide the structure of a database from users.

Views: This is a query that acts like a filter or a window to an underlying table. It has rows and columns just like a table. Views act as a middleman between the user and the table, ensuring a sort of security buffer by hiding the structure of the table from end users. The purpose is so that end users are not able to change the structure of the table or delete the table. Views can also be used to represent a subset of data from multiple tables.

Functions: These are saved expressions that can be used for common tasks in a database. A function can be used in changing the format of a person's name from lowercase letters to proper case, where the first letter of each word is capitalized.

Triggers: Triggers are special types of stored procedures that automatically execute in response to an event that occurs in the database.

Database Terms

Now that database objects and languages and the two categories of databases (OLTP and OLAP) have been explained, let's explore how database technologies are applied. As many as four or five of the terms in this section can be found in any database-related job requisition; as a result, it becomes essential for a technical recruiter to become familiar with the terms and how they are used in the database work environment.

Business Intelligence

Business Intelligence (BI) is the knowledge derived from in-depth analysis of an organization's business data, usually stored in a data warehouse. In some cases, business intelligence is a classier name for a robust reporting system. I cannot talk enough about reporting; what good is an information system if it cannot be reported on?

Take, for instance, the kind of decision you make at the end of the year or beginning of the next year when your credit card company sends you a summary of your spending habits. You will see from looking at it that you spent too much money at a particular retailer or that going to the movies and other entertainment choices costs you too much. Now, what do you do based on this report? You make a DECISION based on this information. For example, you decide to visit the movie house less in the coming year or that you will cut down on your clothing purchases. These are very simple implementations of how a good reporting system can help you make decisions. Now imagine how important business intelligence can be to a major retailer or gas dispensing company.

Data collection is a waste of time if it's not being properly analyzed. When analyzed properly, it helps an online retailer know, for instance:

1. Why on certain days, its sales are higher or lower.
2. Why they sell more of a product than the others, or the factors that may surround this notion.
3. Where the most traffic comes from.
4. Why people abandon the shopping cart just before a purchase.
5. Where shoppers go to from their Web site.
6. The demographics of the purchasers that like a certain type of product.

The retailer sees in its data how people that purchase a particular product end up purchasing another product on the same visit. So what does the retailer do with this information? The retailer may take two product placement actions: (1) place the second product in close proximity with the first, and (2) ensure that the inventory levels on these two products are replenished together.

Another example of this business decision practice that's based on database reporting or business intelligence is what you see at Amazon.com. When a user selects to purchase one book, there's a listing of other books similar to that one, usually with information like "people that purchased this book also purchased these other great books." What better product placement is there? This same implementation is seen in online dating sites: "if you like this person, then you will like these other persons."

Back to the applicant tracking database. If you're reviewing a set of candidates, then you might want to check out other candidates living in close proximity to each other that fit the same criteria. To be able to do this, the data must be collected and stored in separate attributes (skills set, location, and job type for applicant tracking). These are the attributes that when collected and put together create a profile that makes it easy for the end user to decide on what they want quickly.

The typical job titles for the Business Intelligence and Reporting Analyst are Business Intelligence Analyst, Business Intelligence Specialist, SQL Reporting Analyst, and Data Reporting Analyst. The Business Intelligence or Database Reporting Analyst must know the business and understand the flow of data (where it comes from, how it is manipulated, and where it ends up) in order to create decision support or business intelligence systems. This person should have a good understanding of the database languages—T-SQL, PL/SQL, and MySQL—and also the reporting or business intelligence applications used by the company.

Often you will see the BI or reporting person graduate to the position of a database developer. This frequently happens in companies where the reporting analyst feels unglorified, like a class or two lower than their database developer counterparts. In reality, the reporting person is equally as important, if not more important, because he creates the metrics that check to see if a particular implementation was successful or not. These metrics measure the current revenue stream compared to the month/week before the new implementation.

Some BI positions require personnel to have a statistics background. The people with this background tend to find more trends in data. This is not to say that people without this background do not make great analysts.

Database Reporting

Though the impact of reporting in an organization has been explained in the context of business intelligence, it's still worth noting that reporting has its own separate knowledge base and skills sets. An organization may have a good reporting system without implementing the enhanced tools that create the business intelligence aspect.

In a case like this, reporting is the ability to analyze data in order to answer simple questions such as "Of the people that registered on the Web site, how many live in Dallas and are male?"At the very least, every database system should have a good reporting and search functionality. Think of your applicant tracking software that's built on a database system. The ability to search and find candidates in this system with the skills you desire is the simplest implementation of reporting.

Though reporting sounds simple, you may still see bad implementations of it in some software applications. An example is in a case where you have a dozen candidates that have C# skills. You are sure of this because you entered some of the candidates in the system yourself.

You receive a new requisition that requires a C# developer, but cannot seem to retrieve the candidates. Frustrating, yes? On one hand, this is an example of a poor reporting system. On the other, you cannot always blame the inability to retrieve data from a reporting system on the application. Retrieving information from a database system requires good knowledge of the data structure. This is why reporting candidates require time (sometimes as much as two weeks) to acclimatize themselves with data structure, objects, and business rules in order to start reporting.

A good reporting system is very important to any organization. Business determinations and decisions are made from information gathered from database systems. These types of business decisions include deciding to fund the creation of new software for a software company or to create a new flight route for airline companies.

All these actions taken by different companies are backed by information they gathered from their database reporting systems with the help of the reporting analysts and business intelligence analysts (see next chapter for their skills sets). Though we talk about the reporting analyst skills set in the next chapter, one of the questions a recruiter might consider asking a reporting analyst is, "Describe a time when, as a result of your business and data reporting, a change was made by the organization's decision makers."

CALL NOTES

"Describe a time when, as a result of your business and data reporting, a change was made by the organization's decision makers."

Data Mining

This is the process of knowledge discovery or retrieval of hidden information from stored data. Data can be mined whether it is stored in spreadsheets or database tables. The important criterion for the data is not the storage format, but how it applies to the problem to be solved. It is the process of sifting through large amounts of data to produce data relationships, patterns, or trends that might be of value to the organization for producing models and forecasting.

Data mining retailers, like Starbucks and Wal-Mart, may notice the buying pattern of their customers and then make decisions toward better product placements. For example, a business problem might be: "How can a retailer sell more of one product to its customers?" This will be translated into a data mining problem, such as: "Which customers are most likely to purchase the product?" A model that predicts who is most likely to purchase the product must be built on data that describes the customers who have purchased the product in the past.

Before building the model, the retailer must assemble the data that is likely to contain relationships between customers who have purchased the product and customers who have not purchased the product. Customer attributes might include age, number of children, years of residence, owners/renters, and so on.

Database High Availability/Clustering

This is defined as a database system designed for continuous operation in the event of a failure of one or more components. Failover clustering is where there is an automatic transfer of operation from a failed component to a similar, redundant component to ensure uninterrupted flow; this process is done without requiring human intervention.

ETL

Extract, Transform, and Load (ETL) is a process of loading data into a data warehouse or data integration with legacy systems. It involves three steps: extracting data from outside or different sources, transforming it to fit business needs, and then loading it into a database or data warehouse. Figure 9.1 illustrates the steps in the ETL process and how it starts with extracting and ends with loading.

Figure 9.1. Extraction, transformation, and loading.

Data Integration

This is the process of extracting, transforming, and loading ETL data from heterogeneous or diverse data systems. In a company where data sources can come from different databases, the ETL process can be used to extract, transform, and load diverse data from its original location to its intended destination.

Data Partitioning

Partitioning enables tables and indexes to be split into smaller, more manageable components and is a key requirement for any large database with high performance and high availability requirements. Figure 9.2 illustrates how data in the Orders table can be partitioned into several groups of data based on the dates.

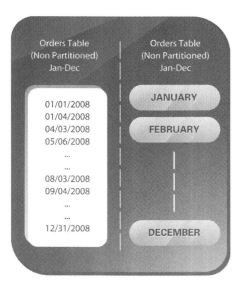

Figure 9.2. Table partitioning.

Database Normalization

Normalization is a logical database design process that involves using formal methods to separate data into multiple, related tables to reduce redundant data, thus creating more disk space and making the table more flexible and consistent. Reasonable normalization frequently improves performance because only related data are stored in a table, which makes it easier and quicker to retrieve data. De-normalization, which is the opposite, is the process of optimizing the performance of a database by adding redundant data. The process of de-normalization is used in specific implementations such as data warehouse.

Data Replication

Replication is a technology for copying and distributing data and database objects from one database to another and then synchronizing these databases to maintain consistency. By using replication, you can distribute data to different locations and to remote or mobile users by means of local and wide area networks, dial-up connections, wireless connections, and the Internet.

Data Warehouse

A data warehouse (DW) is a read-only repository for an organization's historical data. It contains the raw data for management's decision support system. Data mining functions are performed on the data warehouse by data analysts to find business trends.

An organization may use the information stored in its data warehouse to find out what day of the week a particular product was most sold in December 2005. It provides a multidimensional view of an organization's data for analysis. A data warehouse is known for its slowness, but a good DW design is performed in such a way that information is retrieved without bringing the server to a complete stop. Software companies with data warehouse solutions include IBM, NCR, Teradata, SAS, Oracle, and Microsoft.

Data Modeling

Data modeling is the process of designing the structure and flow of data within a given system. Examples of data modeling are logical data modeling, physical data modeling, and architectural data modeling. Some companies that make modeling software for systems design and generation include Embarcadero with its ER/Studio product, Computer Associates with its ERWin product, and Oracle Corporation with its Oracle Designer 10g product. Data modeling is used for creating a high-level description and overview of the properties that make up the flow of data in an information system.

UML (Unified Modeling Language)

UML is the industry standard language for specifying, visualizing, and documenting the components of a software system. It's used to create a blueprint for the development of a software system. UML is used for business process modeling, systems engineering modeling, and creating organizational structures.

MySQL

MySQL (pronounced MY SEQUEL) is an open source SQL Database Management System that has become very popular for creating Web-based database applications. It acts as the database component of the LAMP (Linux, Apache, MySQL, PHP) Web development solution.

Database Solutions

We'll take a look at two major database solutions companies, Microsoft and Oracle. Their products are very similar to one another. Developers usually choose one or the other to specialize on. You may occasionally find candidates that are very good at both; these would mostly be contractors or consultants not tied to any particular client.

The major difference between these two products is Microsoft's refusal to have any of its products written or run on UNIX- or Linux-based operating systems. They are written and can work only on Microsoft Windows. Oracle's database products can work on Windows, different flavors of UNIX, and Linux; this makes it more versatile and attractive to some companies.

Technology	Microsoft	Oracle
Warehouse	SQL Server 2005/2008	Oracle Database 11g, Oracle Warehouse Builder
Reporting	SQL Server Reporting Services (SSRS)	Oracle Reports 10g Release 2
BI	SQL Server 2005/2008	Oracle BI Suite Enterprise Edition Plus
Mining	SQL Server 2005/2008	Oracle Warehouse Builder, Oracle Data Mining
OLAP	SQL Server Analysis Services (included in SQL Server)	Oracle OLAP (embedded in 11g)
Partitioning	Included in SQL Server	Oracle Database 11g (option)
Data Integration	SQL Server Integration Services (SSIS)	Oracle Data Integrator
SQL Dialect	T-SQL (Transact SQL)	PL/SQL

Table 9.2. Microsoft vs. Oracle's database tools.

All of Microsoft's database tools are included in the one product SQL Server, while Oracle has separate software tools not bundled in the main database application. Looking at Table 9.2, you will see that all the tools in the case of Microsoft are included in its main product.

Microsoft Database Solution

The products included in Microsoft's database system are Database Engine, SQL Server Integration Services, SQL Server Analysis Services (SSAS), SQL Server Reporting Services (SSRS), SQL Server Data Mining, and SQL Server Notification Services.

SQL Server 2005/2008

Microsoft SQL Server is an integrated data management and analysis software that enables organizations to manage information and confidently run business applications. SQL Server ships with several components, including: Integration Services, Analysis Services, Reporting Services, and Notification Services. Figure 9.3 shows the components integrated into SQL Server.

Figure 9.3. SQL server components.

SQL Server Integration Services (SSIS)

SSIS provides the ability to transform diverse data into meaningful information. SSIS is an Extraction, Transformation, and Loading (ETL) tool. It accepts data from multiple simultaneous sources, performs complex transformations, and then presents the data to multiple simultaneous destinations. SSIS can be used not only for large data sets, but also for complex dataflows. The equivalent of SSIS in older versions of SQL is called DTS—Data Transformation Services.

SQL Server Analysis Services (SSAS)

SQL Server 2005 Analysis Services (SSAS) provides online analytical processing (OLAP) and data mining functionality for business intelligence applications and reporting. Analysis Services supports OLAP by allowing the design, creation, and management of multidimensional structures that contain data aggregated from other data sources. For data mining applications, Analysis Services enables the design, creation, and visualization of data mining models.

SQL Server Reporting Services (SSRS)

SQL Server Reporting Services is a comprehensive, server-based solution that enables the creation, management, and delivery of both traditional, paper-oriented reports and interactive, Web-based reports. An integrated part of the Microsoft Business Intelligence framework, Reporting Services combines the data management capabilities of SQL Server and Microsoft Windows Server with familiar and powerful Microsoft Office System applications to deliver real-time information to support daily operations and drive decisions.

SQL Server Data Mining

Microsoft SQL Server data mining is part of its family of business intelligence technologies that, when combined, create intelligent data mining applications. These technologies include SQL Server 2005 Integration Services, SQL Server 2005 Analysis Services, and SQL Server Reporting Services. SQL Server includes a built-in Data Mining Wizard and Designer. Figure 9.4 shows the stages of data mining and ETL and how data sources can originate from different applications, such as sales, database, or legacy applications, and still come together into one data warehouse environment to be used in reports or business intelligence purposes.

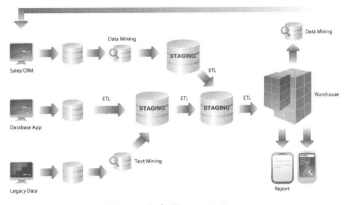

Figure 9.4. Data mining.

SQL Server Notification Services

SQL Server 2005 Notification Services is a platform for developing and deploying applications that generate and send personalized notifications to users. With Notification Services, developers can quickly build notification applications that send timely, personalized information updates, helping to enhance customer relationships.

Oracle Database Solution

Oracle Database Server 11g

This is the database server engine. Oracle provides users and companies more flexibility by developing their database solutions on multiple platforms—UNIX, Windows, and Linux—while Microsoft SQL Server runs only on Windows. Oracle database servers come with several options to meet each organization's requirements for performance, high availability, security, and management. Some of these application options are described below.

Oracle Real Application Clusters

Oracle Real Application Clusters (Oracle RAC), first introduced in Oracle 9i, is included as an option to Oracle Database 11g database server; it supports the deployment of a single database across a cluster of servers. This provides fault tolerance (database is still operational even when a part fails) and scalability (potential for growth). Oracle RAC extends Oracle Database so that you can store, update, and efficiently retrieve data using multiple database instances on different servers at the same time. Oracle RAC provides the software that facilitates servers working together in what is called a cluster.

Oracle Warehouse Builder

This enables the transformation of raw data, typically in different formats and disparate systems, transforming it into high-quality information that's optimized for business reporting and analytics. It provides the connectors to other systems, such as SAP, Siebel, and PeopleSoft, that perform data profiling and data correction for Oracle applications.

Oracle Partitioning

Partitioning enables tables and indexes to be split into smaller, more manageable components and is a key requirement for any large database with high performance and high availability requirements. Oracle Partitioning is an option on the Oracle Database 11*g* Enterprise Edition.

Oracle Data Mining

Oracle Data Mining is an optional product that can be purchased outside of the main database engine, Edition, which enables customers to build integrated business intelligence applications that identify trends and patterns.

Oracle OLAP

Oracle OLAP is an engine that analyzes data from a data warehouse for business processes, such as forecasting, planning, and what-if analysis. It helps businesses identify key trends and model complex business scenarios. This is fully integrated into the Oracle Database, which means that there is no administration learning curve as is typically associated with stand-alone OLAP servers. Organizations can leverage their existing DBA/DBE staff, rather than invest in specialized administration skills.

What We Learned

- Database applications are built based on their need to perform either Online Transaction Processing or Online Analytical Processing—Decision Support.
- The official database language is SQL, declared as a standard by ANSI in 1986.

o   There are three main language categories of SQL: data manipulation language (DML), data definition language (DDL), and data control language (DCL).

- Database objects are the tangible components that make up a database. A few of them are:
  o   Tables, which contain rows and columns that store the attributes of an item.
  o   Stored procedures, which are programmatic objects that are executed automatically and used to validate data, control database access, and return database results.
  o   Views, which are queries that act like filters to an underlying table.
  o   Functions, which are saved expressions that can be used for common tasks in a database.

- Database technologies terms to consider while recruiting for database specialists include:
  o   Business intelligence
  o   Database reporting
  o   Data mining
  o   Database high availability/clustering
  o   Data integration
  o   Data partitioning
  o   Database normalization
  o   Data replication
  o   Extraction, Transformation, and Loading (ETL)
  o   Data warehouse
  o   Data modeling

Chapter 10

Database Job Roles

In This Chapter

- Database administration
- Database development
- Database Engineer (DBE)
- Database Administrator (DBA)
- Data Analyst (DA)
- Extraction, Transformation, Loading (ETL) Developer

Database roles are defined by the company that needs the database specialist. A database administrator in one company may include three separate roles: database development, database reporting, and database administration; while in another company, it may involve only one role: the administration of databases.

In the previous chapter, we examined database terms and technologies and how they are utilized. In this chapter, the specific job roles for the technologies (discussed in the last chapter) will be highlighted. From the reporting analyst, database developer, database administrator, and business intelligence specialist to the data warehouse consultant, this section will analyze the specific duties and requirements of each role, breaking down their responsibilities.

Also found in this chapter is a breakdown of the terms and phrases found in the resumes of database specialists. We also examine the types of questions to ask candidates based on the content of their resumes.

Database Administration

Database Administration (DBA) is the support, maintenance, and management of a database system. The tasks involved are usually process-driven, ranging from system configuration and break-fix to acquiring new hardware. A few years back, some companies combined the tasks of database administration and database development together and sought to find candidates who could perform both.

Even the certification for database technologies combined both development and administration. An example was the Microsoft Certified Database Administrator (MCDBA), which included exams for both disciplines. Today, though you may find the occasional "SQL Developer/ DBA" job titles, most companies now know to separate these disciplines. These roles really should be separate because the innate skills sets for database administration are different from those of development.

Administration involves configuration, maintenance, and troubleshooting, while development involves programming skills. The programmer is more analytic in nature and thinks in process (please note that these skills can also be learned), while the DBA configures systems to work together, manages security and user permissions, configures backup and recovery, and sometimes optimizes the database objects to ensure optimal performance.

Most companies are now choosing to separate the database administration and database development roles. Candidates are also doing the same, choosing to focus their skills where they are most challenged and rewarded.

Database Development

The process of designing "*containers*" that collect different attributes of a system is the job of a database developer. A database developer with a good understanding of the business requirements defines the kinds of data attributes that must be collected, and also the relationships between one attribute and the others. The database developer writes the process for collecting this data. This data collection process is similar to what you find when a candidate goes to a company's job site and is led through a process of selecting a job and then filling out data such as first name, last name, skills sets, education, location, and so on. The database developer also writes code that fulfills business rules and requirements. An example of this is when a database developer includes a process that triggers an action when a blacklisted e-mail address or IP address is detected during a Web form registration.

Study of a Database-Related Job Description

Job descriptions tell a recruiter the skills sets sought after by a company; they also contain clues as to the technical environment found in the company. In this section we study a database-specific job description—Database Developer—where the database terms and their uses in this particular position are expounded. The duties and responsibilities will also be explained. It's always easier to identify the needs and wants of a hiring manager by underlining or highlighting specific skills sets. In Figure 10.1, some of the duties and responsibilities have been underlined. The underlined terms will be explained in the section below.

Database Developer

Provide expert database design, development, and implementation using Microsoft SQL Server 2008.

Duties and Responsibilities:
1. Develop and document data migration strategies and ETL plans.
2. Develop complex SQL scripts to support other development teams.
3. *Optimize and tune* SQL statements and databases.
4. Perform database infrastructure design and automation of data loads.
5. Troubleshoot and resolve database issues.
6. Manage the database development, quality assurance, and production database environments and manage application upgrades on them.
7. Support internal clients by creating data-driven applications/reports and ad hoc queries.

Qualifications and Requirements:
1. B.S. in Computer Science, Mathematics, or Engineering.
2. 4+ years experience working as a database developer with SQL Server.
3. Experience in SQL Server <u>DTS/SSIS</u>.
4. Must have demonstrated understanding of <u>logical</u> and <u>physical database design</u> for <u>transactional</u>, <u>data warehouse</u>, and data (de) <u>normalization</u> concepts.
5. Deep knowledge and proven experience working in advanced T-SQL.
6. Experience with SQL Server 2008 Reporting services.
7. Experience in business <u>requirement analysis</u> and conversion to database design.
8. Experience with <u>business intelligence</u> products such as Business Objects or Cognos.

Figure 10.1. Typical job description for SQL Server Developer.

Responsibilities Analysis

Having been on both sides of the recruiting spectrum—as a candidate and also as a technical recruiter, I know that it's imperative for a technical recruiter to understand the reason behind a company's need for specific skills. The recruiter that understands the needs of the hiring manager (and candidate) wins the respect of both the candidates and hiring managers. This recruiter is able to communicate better with the candidates, able to identify at the outset when a candidate does (not) meet the required needs. The candidate, in turn, will respect the recruiter's grasp of the client's technology environment and is more open to the recruiter.

With this in mind, the following pages analyze and describe the skills sets found in database developer job descriptions and why companies may require these skills.

Data Migration is the process of copying or moving data from one database system to another. The movement of data may be from disparate systems, such as from Access to SQL, or may be from similar systems, such as from one SQL Server database to another SQL Server database. The process of migration is not complete until the data has been tested or validated to ensure its integrity and reliability. So the database developer has to develop scripts (e.g., checksum scripts) to run on the migrated data to validate its reliability.

Why? Part of a database developer's task deals with knowing where data originates from, where it ends up, and how to manipulate the data to fit the organization's requirements. Sometimes the data he works with may be stored in another format and in another database; the database developer must know how to move or migrate this data from one point to the other. There's always more than one way to perform a task, so the developer for this position must be able to document a best-practice strategy for performing this task in his organization.

ETL is the process of extracting, transforming, and loading data from disparate sources to its destination source. A migration process (previously described) can also include ETL processes.

Why? The developer should have experience extracting and transforming data from different sources and then loading it into the destination database table(s).

Tuning and optimizing: Just like a car has to go through periodic tuning by a mechanic that understands the internal workings, so it is with a database system; after a period of continuous smooth running, the database objects need some tuning. Sometimes the tuning may be as a result of initial bad design, in which case the developer corrects it, or it may only involve the tweaking of some objects to make them perform better.

Why? Databases like Oracle Database or Microsoft SQL Server come with tools that enable a person to optimize or tune the database. The developer needs to know how to use these tools to tune database objects.

Infrastructure design is the process of defining and creating the source, destination, interdependability, and connectivity of all moving parts of a particular database solution. The developer defines diagrammatically the source, destination, and relationship of all the tables, views, stored procedures, triggers, and replication involved in a given solution.

Why? It's crucial that the developer knows how to design a solution from beginning to end—more so for a developer that is familiar with the data environment than for a developer who just started at a company.

Automation of data loads involves the use of DTS—Data Transformation Services (in SQL 2000) or SSIS—SQL Server Integration Services (in

SQL 2005) to load data into database tables. These tools can be used to automate the process of locating the data source, *extracting* the raw data, *transforming* (scrubbing) it to an acceptable format, and then *loading* it into the database.

Why? All the processes involved in migrating, transforming, and loading data can be automated with tools. Being able to use these tools to perform these tasks will save time and reduce the load on the database server. This skill is seen as a core requirement for any database developer.

Qualifications Analysis

DTS/SSIS: DTS means Data Transformation Services, which is an ETL tool in SQL Server 2000, and SSIS means SQL Server Integration Services, which is the enhanced ETL tool in SQL Server 2005. This is a core skill requirement.

Logical database design: The logical design of the database is the implementation of tables and the relationships between them. This is a core requirement for creating relational databases. A good logical database design can lay the foundation for optimal database and application performance. A poor logical database design can hinder the performance of the whole system.

Physical database design : This describes how a database system will be physically implemented in order to meet its logical requirements. The performance of any database depends on the effective configuration of the physical design structures, including indexes, clustered indexes, indexed views, and partitions. The purpose of these physical structures is to enhance the performance and manageability of databases.

(De)Normalizing: This is performed during the logical database design. It involves using methods to separate data into multiple related tables. When designed properly, normalization improves database performance.

Requirements analysis: This is the determination of the needs and conditions to be met for a new or updated system. This analysis is usually documented in a use case and/or product specifications document. The database developer often designs a database based on this document.

Database Role Descriptions

A look at different database technology roles in Table 10.1 reveals how each role manipulates the same objects to fit their job function. Though the Data Analyst works with the same objects as the developer, she does so in a different capacity and for a different purpose. This purpose defines the design and data manipulation considerations of each role. Table 10.1 differentiates the database roles and can be used in managing the transition of candidates from one role to another.

	Database Engineer (DBE)	Database Administrator (DBA)	ETL Developer	Data (Report) Analyst
Overall Database	Designs database solutions using tables, stored procedures, functions, views, and indexes.	Maintenance of database systems in production environment.	Extracts data from one system, scrubs and transforms the data to fit destination table, and then loads same data.	Writes reports/ queries from data stored in tables.
Environment	Works in development and testing environments. These are internal noncustomer-facing systems.	Works in production environment. This is external customer-facing system.	Works in the data warehouse environment. Internal noncustomer-facing system.	Works in the report environment. Internal noncustomer-facing system.
Stored Procedures	Designs procedures that insert data into tables; updates or deletes data already in tables.	May write and execute procedures that perform database tuning and maintenance.	Creates stored procedures that automate the process of extracting, scrubbing, or loading data	Writes procedures that "select" data stored in tables. Does not update or delete data he/she is reporting from.

Tables	Creates many tables to store data required for the solution at hand.	Maintains tables created by the DBE in the production environment.	Creates many tables to store data in between loads and in the data warehouse solution.	May create several tables to store subsets of data for analysis.
Performance Tuning	Optimizes and tunes database objects in order that they perform better and faster.	Carries out any further optimization required in the production environment.	Optimizes database objects used in the ETL process.	Optimizes the database objects used in running reports.

Table 10.1. Database roles.

Everyone involved in database administration, development, integration, or reporting has created databases; stored procedures, functions, views, tables, and indexes; and sometimes even created replications scripts using Data Manipulation Language (DML) and Data Definition Language (DDL). But the question here is, *"Where is their focus?"*

A person whose primary function is on administration cannot be confused with a developer or a data analyst. So we try to differentiate their focus so it becomes clearer to the technical recruiter what to look for when reviewing all the resumes that come in for any of the positions.

There used to be a blur between the tasks of the DBA and the DBE, but currently, with highly specialized skills sets in either job, the blur has minimized and maybe even disappeared. That said, there are still some companies that maintain job descriptions that include skills sets of both the DBE and the DBA. Independent school districts or smaller companies are good examples of organizations that may not have the need for both a full-time DBA and a full-time DBE. This is because there isn't much work to require these two positions. So the solution is to have one person perform both tasks. Though some candidates can perform both, it's not a generally acceptable scenario.

Database Engineer (DBE)

Main Attributes: Designs database solutions that solve problems with the use of stored procedures, tables, indexes, and replication. The DBE's tasks revolve around creating stored procedures that interact with underlying tables to enter data into tables, delete data, or change data.

The following are some of the considerations a DBE might make for creating a database centric application.

o   Ninety percent of the DBE's tasks revolve around writing database code. The other 10 percent is on managing expectations. The DBE is always busy managing builds and releases in the development, quality assurance, and production environments. The DBE works with the configuration manager to ensure that the most recent and tested code is propagated to the production environment.

o   The DBE also has a lot of interaction with software testers/quality assurance analysts. The DBA, on the other hand, has little interaction with software testing; DBAs don't write enough code to require that much testing.

o   The DBE is interested in the performance of the database objects she created. The DBE will use statements like *"performed query optimization, index tuning, and custom replication to improve database performance"* during interviews and in their resumes.

RESUME PHRASES   Database Engineer

Designed and implemented a highly normalized membership registration database that contained approximately 1000 stored procedures and 300 tables. Created custom replication scripts of production databases to the reporting and read servers.

Keywords of note: design database solution, custom replication, stored procedure

---

Figure 10.2. Phrases in a Database Engineer's resume.

The Real-World DBE

To build a simple registration and membership solution, the real-world DBE will create the "member" table, with fields that store the attributes of each member as the member registers. The DBE will also write code to verify that usernames and e-mail addresses are not duplicated by members; she will determine how to store a member's uncompleted registration data when the member abandons a form. The DBE will also write code to remember the member the next time s(he) comes back to complete registration. In the code, the DBE verifies the completeness and accuracy of data before it's entered into the table.

Figure 10.3 depicts an example of the business requirements a developer determines in order to build a photo upload system.

Janet was tasked to design a photo upload system at the company where she worked as a database developer. Some business requirements may include:

1. A person can upload one to ten (1–10) photos.
2. The maximum upload for a basic user is three (3).
3. After three (3) photos, the user is asked to upgrade subscription.
4. Photos must be good quality and inoffensive (this means the photo must go through an approval process).

Developer's Design Process:

1. The developer will design the tables that store the users' photo information; this must be tied to the users' membership table to check their subscription levels.
2. There must be a counter in place to check the number of photos uploaded.
3. There must be a process that fires once a basic user tries to upload the fourth photo.
4. There must be an approval application process that checks to ensure photos are inoffensive (this may be a manual process).

Figure 10.3. Real-life example of a database developer's tasks.

Looking at the four business requirements from Figure 10.3, you can see that the database developer has a lot on their hands. Your job as a technical recruiter is to ensure that the developer you refer to your client has had demonstrated experience creating database applications based on requirements, and can articulate the process involved in actually designing and creating database objects.

During the design process for the above real-life project, the developer must have identified all the data inputs, where data will be coming from, where the processed data will end up, and how the data may be utilized by other processes. If this is the case, then the candidate (developer) would find it easy to describe this process to the recruiter.

Depending on what your client is looking for—junior-, mid-, or senior-level developer—your objective is to ensure you speak with the candidate to describe a solution they had created and the thinking that went into this creation or development. If you ask a database developer to describe the design of a product that she developed and the problem she was trying to fix, she will be able to describe the process if in fact she worked on it.

If you mow your lawn every so often, you can describe the process of performing that impossible task! The same is true for a developer or administrator that has performed a task numerous times: that candidate will be able to describe the process of performing that task with reasonable ease. The opposite may be true for a person that has not performed a task.

As a technical recruiter, you must also bear in mind that some candidates tend to forget to mention details as a result of their familiarity with a process. If you perform a task every day, it comes so naturally that you forget the details of the task when trying to explain it to someone else.

Recruiter Conversation with a Database Engineer

The following are some questions a technical recruiter might ask a database engineer in order to understand their focus. Most technical candidates feel that recruiters do not have much knowledge about the intricacies of their technical skills, so this is why we start this recruiter-to-candidate conversation with a tone that makes the candidate feel like they can actually relate to the recruiter.

QUESTIONS

The recruiter may start by going through the preliminaries of basic recruiter and candidate greetings and afterward flow right into the interview.

Greeting:
"Hi. My name is Helen Olive from ABC Solution. I saw your resume online and wanted to find out more about your skills sets in relation to a position I have today.... Is this okay?"

Interview:
"I enjoy listening to how programmers solve business problems with code. I'm going to ask you some general questions; your answers will give me a better understanding of what you do and perhaps what you enjoy the most in your job. Is that okay with you?"

a) *"Please describe your database environment... your development, testing, and perhaps production environments."*

b) *"Within SQL Server database, there are tools and tasks that include SSIS, SSRS, notification services, replication, performance tuning, and the design of the database solution. Which of these activities do you enjoy the most?"*

c) *"Which of the SQL Server tools do you use on a day-to-day basis and for what types of solution?"*

d) *"Describe a database application or feature you developed or assisted in developing; what problems did that application or feature solve? What were the considerations for this feature or design?"*

e) *"What is the frequency of code propagation to your production environment?"*

The above questions, as you may notice, are all Microsoft SQL Server centric. These tools and experiences can be replaced to suit other database technologies where applicable. The questions here are designed to reveal the experience level of the developer and match their experiences with the requirements of the hiring manager.

The following are the reasons you asked these questions in the first place.

Reason for question a: This tells the recruiter about the database environment, the size of the team, if this was a two-person or twenty-person database development team, if a process was followed for development—like SDLC or any other process. It will also give the recruiter a view to finding out if the candidate understands the inner working of the development team. The answers here should include how many servers were available in the testing and production environments. The answer should also include the platform supported, whether it was Windows, UNIX, both, or another combination.

Reason for question b: With the exception of SSRS, the answers here should include all the tools and tasks outlined in this question. These are all core tasks for the DBE. The SSRS is really a reporting tool, usually used by the reporting or data analyst.

Reason for question c: The answers here should include how at least one of the tasks in the former question was performed. For example, the candidate would explain how he/she implemented replication or performance tuning and how this solved a business problem.

Reason for question d: The answers here should include at least one feature (no matter how small) that the candidate has been in charge of starting and completing. The answer format should look like or sound like the one found in Figure 10.3.

Reason for question e: The answers here should tell you the pace of the candidate's current or past organization and what pace he/she is more comfortable with. Whether the frequency was once/twice a week or once a month, the answer will also highlight if the candidate is open to and enjoys a fast pace or prefers family time and some level of order.

Database Administrator (DBA)

Main Attributes: AKA Production DBA. This DBA's main focus is in the administration of the database—its availability, security, and accessibility, among other factors. The DBA will tell you the size of database administered and how many servers they managed. This does not mean that the DBE is not interested in this aspect, but it just shows you the candidate's primary focus.

The DBA will mention how many boxes or servers she *administered* and the types of server used for this (whether it's DELL, HP, etc.). This will be displayed with phrases like, *"Administered 20 back-end SQL Servers; managed database backup and restore, user permissions, DTS/SSIS Packages, and replication jobs; performed operating system updates and security fixes on QA environment server."* The DBE is not interested in this—not that she does not know if you ask her, but again, that's not the focus for the DBE. The words "configured" and "configuration" are very common in the DBA's resume. "Planning & Implementation" and "monitoring" are also very important to the DBA.

The following are some of the considerations a DBA might make for planning and maintaining a 24/7 database application.

o   The DBA's tasks revolve around planning, installation, configuration, backup, and maintenance of database servers in a production environment. She works with systems administrators to configure best-practice security and high availability database systems.

o   The DBA works with configuration managers and systems administrators to ensure that the most recent and tested code is propagated to the production environment.

o   The DBA is most interested in the performance and optimization of database objects in the production environment.

RESUME PHRASES   Database Administrator

Performed capacity planning for memory and space. Performed database consistency checks using the DBCC stored procedures. Responsible for the installation, upgrade, and configuration of all company SQL Servers. Planned, executed, and maintained database installations, upgrades, service packs, security patches, and scheduled database tasks. Managed user accounts and assigned permissions. Performed replication and log shipping. Established and implemented database backup and recovery policies and practices. Monitored data and log file growth, disk utilization, memory, and CPU.

Keywords of note: optimization, log shipping, replication, mirroring, backup/recovery

---

Figure 10.4. Phrases in a Database Administrator's resume.

The Real-World DBA

To create a highly available database system, the DBA has several options to consider from log shipping (automated process of backing up, copying, and restoring logs from one database to another) and replication (copying and distributing data and database objects from one to many other databases) to mirroring (maintaining a warm/hot standby database server that can be automatically activated once there is a failure with the original server). The DBA can configure all three options depending on the database environment and the needs of the organization.

Figure 10.5 depicts an example of the business requirements a DBA determines in order to implement a highly available database system.

Mark was tasked to implement a highly available database system in support of the organization's need for 24/7 data availability. Some requirements may include:

1. Maintain a duplicate copy of the database.
2. Automatic failover to another server upon failure of primary database.
3. No data lag should exist between the primary and secondary databases.

Administrator's implementation process includes:

1. The DBA will consider implementing database mirroring, traditional backup/restore, replication, or log shipping.
2. The DBA will choose mirroring because this technology is the only one that offers automatic failover amid the other SQL Server solutions.
3. Mirroring also ensures that there is no latency or data lag between the primary and secondary database server.

Figure 10.5. Real-life example of a database administrator's tasks.

Looking at the three business requirements from Figure 10.5, the database administrator has to understand what each of the three implementation processes can and cannot offer in order to make a determination on which is the better solution, or whether to combine the implementation solutions for an even more robust environment.

So it's not enough for a technical recruiter to accept "*Yes, I have experience configuring database mirroring*"; the recruiter also has to understand from the candidate's perspective the business requirements that necessitated the need for implementing mirroring. This knowledge will not only sure up the candidate's skills for the recruiter but also help the recruiter understand more of the use of the technology being recruited for.

Recruiter Conversation with a Database Administrator

The following are some questions a technical recruiter might ask a database administrator to understand their experience level and fit.

QUESTIONS

The recruiter may start by going through the preliminaries of basic recruiter and candidate greetings and afterward flow right into the interview.

Greeting:
"Hi. My name is Helen Olive from ABC Solution. I saw your resume online and wanted to find out more about your skills sets in relation to a position I have today.... Is this okay?"

Interview:
"I'm going to ask you some general questions; your answers will give me a better understanding of what you do and perhaps what you enjoy the most in your job as a database administrator. Is that okay?"

   a) *"Please describe your production database environment; how many database servers you administer, how many people are in your group, and who you report to."*
   b) *"What database technologies have been implemented in your environment—such as mirroring, replication, snapshot, log shipping? How do you use each of these technologies? If there's an issue/problem with any of these implemented technologies in your organization, how does it affect your organization?"*
   c) *"Is there a separation of tasks between database development and administration in your current/past organization? Do you find yourself doing the DBA as well as the DBE work? Which of these would you rather be doing?"*
   d) *"Regarding performance tuning, describe a performance issue that you helped resolve. What tools or combination of tools did you use?"*

These questions, as you may have noticed, are designed to reveal the experience level of the database administrator and match their experiences with the requirements of the hiring manager.

The following are the reasons you asked these questions in the first place.

Reason for question a: The answer to this question will tell you a lot about the candidate's current environment. If it's a small one and your job description wants a person who has worked in a large database group, then this might present a small problem. It becomes less of an issue when you understand why the hiring manager wants a DBA with large group experience. If there's no explanation and your candidate has all the other needed skills, then the onus is on you, the recruiter, to make your case that your candidate is a good fit.

The main differences between persons with experience in large groups versus small groups is that the large group candidate has experience working in silos, and he understands bureaucracy requirements, knows to get written permission for every major task, and can accept doing the same tasks every day without frustration. The small group candidate, on the other hand, knows little about bureaucracy and may require daily work challenges in order to stay with the company.

Reason for question b: The answer to this question will give you a better understanding of the technologies used in the candidate's organization and the part played by the candidate in implementing these technologies. The second part of the question will also give you (the recruiter) information on the candidate's troubleshooting inclination.

Reason for question c: The answer to this question will let you know the direction and type of organization the candidate currently works with. These days, organizations separate the tasks of the DBA from DBE. When organizations combine the two, it's a clear indication that the organization does not need a specialized administrator or developer; they probably only need a SQL Server database specialist.

The skills combination is also an indication that the organization is probably not a software development company; the company is mostly charged with the maintenance of a database system that supports an internally used software application.

Reason for question d: Performance tuning is a major skill requirement for most DBA work. Most DBAs with more than a year's experience may have encountered a performance issue at one time or the other. You want to hear of one such experience and the part the candidate played in resolving the issue.

Data Analyst

Main Attributes: AKA Report Analyst, Database Analyst, Business System Analyst, SQL Server Data Analyst, Oracle Database Analyst. The Data Analyst is a combination of the business analyst and the report writer. The business analyst skills that come into play for the Data Analyst are: the ability to perform requirements gathering from business units to find out the kinds of information needed for decision making; the ability to work closely with different departments to define, develop, and deploy reports; and a good understanding of the organization's business—how it works and the flow of information and finances.

The bottom line for every profit-based organization is the ability to increase revenue year after year. To enable this growth, the organization must recognize what works and what doesn't for their customers and users. The job of the Data Analyst is to find trends that highlight what works and what does not and present them in reports to the business decision makers.

The following are some of the considerations a Data Analyst might make for planning and writing reports for an online subscription application.

- o Establish the demographics of paid subscribers versus nonsubscribers—their locations, gender, marital status, age group, and other interests.
- o Ascertain the money trail; track the number of first-time subscriptions versus registrations.
- o Find out the average number of registrations that converted to paid subscriptions.
- o Recognize trends that affect the viability of an organization's product and then create reports that provide the information to business decision makers.
- o Review and analyze detailed business requirements that help in producing monthly/weekly reporting.

RESUME PHRASES   Data Analyst

Trends analysis, data analysis, business requirements, scheduled report delivery, ad hoc reports, SQL Server Reporting Services (SSRS), Oracle reports, write SQL queries with SQL Server T-SQL or Oracle PL/SQL, data extraction, data transfer, and data load (using SSIS)

Keywords of note: trends, requirements, SQL, DTS, SSIS

Figure 10.6. Phrases in a Data Analyst's resume.

The Real-World Data Analyst

The Data Analyst must understand the business of the organization in order to detect and analyze trends within data collected by the company. The Data Analyst must also have a keen understanding of relational database concepts and database structure. Knowledge of statistics may also be a major requirement for some organizations.

Figure 10.7 depicts an example of the business requirements a Data Analyst determines in order to answer business questions.

Victor is tasked with finding out why subscriptions are down considerably every Thursday. Some of the considerations Victor makes may include questions like:

1. Who are the major subscribers, and what are their demographics?
2. Is the low-Thursday-subscriber issue universal?
3. Does it apply in similar subscription products at other organizations, or does this only happen with this client's products?

The data analysis process includes:

1. Using SQL, write statements to collect data to analyze the major subscribing demographics—male, female, age groups, income, etc.
2. Collect data to analyze the subscriber's main interests—TV, sports, social networking, etc.
3. Put the data together to find out what the major subscribing demographics do on Thursdays. This may give an indication of why subscriptions are down on Thursdays.

Figure 10.7. Real-life example of a data analyst's tasks.

Looking at Figure 10.7, we can see that the Data Analyst is asking questions in order to find out the reason for the low subscriber activity on Thursdays.

The focus of this job role is being able to ask business questions—the right ones. These questions are written in SQL statements and executed on the database system; the questions are very many and asked in various ways in order to reveal permutations of possible answers. So in order to ask these various questions of the system, the Data Analyst must have a good understanding of the database language—SQL, the database structure (data stored in each table and how all the tables are related), and the business rules that apply in the database.

The Data Analyst should know how to count, group, and aggregate data. In the case above, the Data Analyst runs a series of queries to select all the subscribers in the database for the previous three months; he groups the data based on gender, age, income, interests, and date and time of subscription. From the result of this query, the Data Analyst can tell the gender group that subscribes the most and their age and income level.

From this query result, the Data Analyst can also run another query to find out the major interests of the subscribers. For the sake of simplicity, let's say the Data Analyst finds out that 89 percent of this subscriber group listed TV watching as an interest; this indicates that they like watching TV. The Data Analyst also finds out that 90 percent of these subscribers subscribed on days other than Thursday. The Data Analyst puts two and two together to arrive at a conclusion: Thursday nights are great TV show nights, and perhaps would-be subscribers prefer watching TV on Thursdays rather than spending time on their computers and the Internet.

Recruiter Conversation with a Data Analyst

Here are some questions a technical recruiter might ask a Data Analyst to understand their experience level, analytic skills, and focus. The recruiter wants to know the database skills of the candidate.

The recruiter may start by going through the preliminaries of basic recruiter and candidate greetings and afterward flow right into the interview.

QUESTIONS

Greeting:
"Hi. My name is Helen Olive from ABC Solution. I saw your resume online and wanted to find out more about your skills sets in relation to a position I have today…. Is this okay?"

Interview:
"I'm going to ask you some general questions; your answers will give me a better understanding of what you do and perhaps what you enjoy the most in your job as a data analyst. Is that okay?"

a.   *"Please describe your database reporting environment—how many reporting servers are available in your environment, the makeup of your team and the platform you support."*

b.   *"How does your reporting environment get refreshed with current data from the production environment? Who in your team performs this task? Is the refresh task automated?"*

c.   *"Do you consider yourself a business data analyst or a data analyst? Why, in either case?"*

d.   *"What business trends have you identified in your database system? Can you describe one and the considerations you made to conclude that this was a trend?"*

e.   *"Do you aspire to move from a role of a data analyst to a SQL developer in the future? Or have you worked as a SQL developer in the past?"*

You may notice that the above questions are designed to reveal the experience level of the data analyst and match their experiences with the requirements of the hiring manager. The following are the reasons these questions are asked.

Reason for question a: The answer to this question brings to light the general data environment, such as the number of servers, type of software, and the size of the data analyst team.

Reason for question b: The answer to this question will highlight the data analyst's understanding of their data environment. There may be three to four database environments in an organization, such as development, quality assurance, staging, production, and reporting/data warehouse environments. Data in the reporting and data warehouse environments comes from production; the process that leads to the flow of data from production to reporting is what the recruiter wants to make sure the data analyst understands and can articulate. The answers can be data replication, backup/restore, snapshot, and so forth.

Reason for question c: The titles business data analyst and data analyst are synonymous to each other; the former just has the business prefix to identify to the candidates that the data analyst should have both business as well as technical inclinations.

Reason for question e: This will tell you their level of skills in SQL Language. If the Data Analyst has never considered himself a SQL developer, it may mean one of two things: a) he likes the data analyst job very much because it combines business as well as technical knowledge and he cannot consider being only a technical person, or b) he is very confident in his SQL skills to even think about the possibility of this upgraded and more technical position. A Data Analyst with experience in creating stored procedures, functions, views, jobs, alerts, and so on will be very comfortable graduating to the developer role. Of course, this opens up another dimension of whether this Data Analyst is really interested in data analysis. Since this was not the original reason this question was asked, we will focus on the reason that was: to ascertain the level of the candidate's SQL skill. You are welcome to ask other follow-up questions that arise as a result of the candidate's answers.

ETL Developer

Main Attributes: The ETL Developer can also be known as the Data Warehouse Developer. Their main focus is in the migration, load, and integration of data into a data warehouse environment. They build database code that populates data from the production environment into the reporting and data warehouse environments. Using tools like SSIS (SQL Server) or SQL*Loader (Oracle), they perform all of the data transformations necessary to populate data into warehouse tables.

The ETL Developer works with different department heads to gather business requirements in order to customize data applications to suit their reporting needs. This process involves data testing, validation, and verification that ensures the integrity of data used for decision making by the various business units.

The ETL Developer must be proficient in the technologies of transferring data from disparate data systems, such as from text files, spreadsheets, Access, and Oracle, into their destination systems, which may be very different from the source.

The following are considerations a Data Warehouse or ETL Developer might make for extracting, transforming, and loading data from a source to the data warehouse destination.

- o As a result of the sheer size of the data in the data warehouse, it is imperative that the developer performs ongoing data warehouse maintenance and performance tuning to analyze query plans, indexes, and locking behavior.
- o Determine if the data that needs transformation is complex. If so, there may be a need for creating SSIS scripts that require VB.Net or C# skills.

RESUME PHRASES   ETL Developer

Data warehouse concepts and best practices, BCP and bulk insert operations in SQL Server, principles and techniques in data warehousing (OLAP, business intelligence (BI), metadata management, multidimensional database, data modeling, and cubes). Experience with data modeling and OLAP tools such as Erwin Data Modeler, SQL Server Analysis Server (SSAS), and Multi Dimensional Expressions (MDX). Experience in SSIS, Query Analyzer, SQL Profiler, Replication, Crystal Reports, TOAD, DBArtisian, ERwin, SQL*Loader.

Keywords of note: ETL, DB modeling, OLAP, metadata, data warehouses

---

Figure 10.8. Phrases in an ETL Developer's resume.

The Real-World ETL Developer

The ETL Developer works with management and development teams to build business intelligence solutions. This person translates decision support business requirements into technical design documents by creating data models that represent dataflow. These data models are developed bearing in mind the scalability and performance needs of a data warehouse system, an ever-increasing data repository.

The ETL Developer creates ETL scripts and processes using SDLC. This person also reviews and tests all ETL scripts and processes (some organizations have an ETL Tester as a separate job role). A big part of the ETL Developer's job is to troubleshoot and tune the data warehouse and decision support applications for optimum performance.

Figure 10.9 depicts an example of the business requirements an ETL Developer determines in order to extract, transform, and load data.

Willy is tasked with extracting, transforming, and loading data received from five different database servers into a Microsoft SQL Server-based data warehouse. Some questions may include:

1. Where is the data coming from, what is the format of the source data, and does it require transformation to fit the destination data?
2. What is the frequency of the data load? Is this a one-time, weekly, or monthly load?
3. Is there an ETL script that could be reused, or will there be a need to create new scripts?
4. How will the data be tested after the load?
5. Will the data form a subset of current data, or will it form its own category?

The ETL process includes:
1. Once the data location and format are identified, use DTS or SSIS tool to create scripts to retrieve identified formatted data from source.
2. If the load is a one-time event, then create a one-time manual script that performs the job. If the frequency is more, the ETL Developer creates automated scripts that run based on a set schedule.
3. After the data is extracted, transformed, and loaded into the target database, the ETL developer tests the data to ensure integrity and accuracy.

Figure 10.9. Real-life example of an ETL Developer's tasks.

Looking at the considerations in Figure 10.9, you can see that the ETL Developer is interested in the source and destination of data, how the data looks, and if it will fit in with what's currently available. The ETL Developer creates scripts that retrieve and load the data from one database to another.

Recruiter Conversation with an ETL Developer

These are some questions a technical recruiter might ask an ETL developer to understand their experience level. After going through the preliminaries of the basic recruiter and candidate exchange, the recruiter may start the conversation using the example below.

QUESTIONS

The recruiter may start by going through the preliminaries of basic recruiter and candidate greetings and afterward flow right into the interview.

Greeting:
"Hi. My name is Helen Olive from ABC Solution. I saw your resume online and wanted to find out more about your skills sets in relation to a position I have today.... Is this okay?"

Interview:
"I'm going to ask you some general questions; your answers will give me a better understanding of what you do and perhaps what you enjoy the most in your job as an ETL developer. Is that okay?"

   a. *"Please describe your data warehouse environment—how many database servers you work with, how many people are in your group, and who you report to."*
   b. *"If your ETL process is documented, please describe what it entails. For instance, if there's new data to be extracted, transformed, and loaded into your database, how you would start this process while adhering to your documented processes?"*

The above questions are designed to reveal the experience level of the ETL developer and match their experiences with the requirements of the hiring manager. The following are the reasons you ask these questions.

Reason for question a: The same as with all the previous job roles, you want to understand the candidate's current work environment.

Reason for question b: The answer to this question reveals if there's a documented process followed for the ETL process, the candidate's understanding of this process, and if the candidate was part of the process development. You will also gain more understanding of the considerations and process of ETL in the candidate's current organization.

What We Learned

- Database administrators (DBAs) are different from database engineers (DBEs). The former is engaged in the administration of the production system, while the latter is a developer/programmer and writes code using database syntax.
- In the study of database-related job descriptions, the responsibilities and qualifications of the database developer and database administrator were analyzed.
- We identified the main differences between the major database roles, from the developer, administrator, analyst, and ETL developer.
- Each job role that was reviewed included the analysis of real-world job tasks and the considerations the people in these roles make for their daily tasks.
- We reviewed a typical recruiter's conversation with the database developer, database administrator, data analyst, and ETL developer.

Chapter 11

Systems Administration

In This Chapter

- o   Network systems management
- o   Systems administration versus systems architect
- o   Application systems administration

Mention the phrase "systems administration," and the top-of-mind visual a person gets is the management of network systems. That's good, but network systems administration is not the only systems administration type available. There is also the administration of application systems, which is the management of enterprise-wide applications used by an organization mostly for running its business processes. The applications may include functions like accounting, finance, payroll, sales, and manufacturing, to name a few. This chapter will deal with both systems administration topics: network systems administration and application systems administration.

Network Systems Administration

Network systems administration refers to enterprise-wide management of distributed computer systems. Systems administration has come a long way: though still thoroughly grounded in the management of hardware, software, access, and the security of the network where these reside, systems administration is now much bigger, more complicated, and—frankly—far more sophisticated than it was five to ten years ago. Today, it has grown beyond the boundaries of managing and administering Local Area Networks (LANs) and Wide Area Networks (WANs) with simple tools to become a considerable force in every organization.

The tasks of a systems administrator depend on the size of the organization. If the organization is small, the systems administrators manage local area networks and local servers with locally attached disks. If the organization is large, then about 50 percent of the systems administrator's time is spent managing network-attached storage and off-site data storage, and justifying the need to acquire more resources. The other 50 percent is spent managing the networking infrastructure between the organization's locations.

Though systems administrators represent desktop and network administration, there is a newer and higher level systems administration referred to as *Infrastructure Architecture*. The growth of this new job description is seen in almost all big organizations, where there is a growing need for strategy thinkers in network design. This need for strategists was usually only found in business development and finance areas, but now a growing number of organizations with large WAN networks see this job title as significantly important as IT continues to be globalized.

Systems administration as a whole has a morph syndrome and will continue to mutate into many titles that are yet to be named. This mutation can easily be identified when a search is run (on any of the popular job sites) with "systems administrator." The resulting job descriptions may contain similar tasks, but the job titles are dissimilar. These new titles depend in part on the hiring organization and the technology landscape. Some morphed titles include systems architect, storage architect, infrastructure architect, network administrator, and a host of other related technology administration roles that originate from the administration of computer systems.

Systems Administration and Infrastructure Architecture

Though the titles Systems Administrator and Infrastructure Architect may involve similar tasks and therefore be used more or less interchangeably, they are really not the same (at least the individuals with the *architect* title do not think the titles are the same).

Systems administration is the setting up, configuration, and maintenance of a particular system. The *Infrastructure Architect* is a well-rounded person with working knowledge of the business as well as technical aspects of the organization. The knowledge base of the architect is usually acquired through experience, education, and a breadth of knowledge in technology and its application in an organization's business.

The main difference here is that the systems administrator homes in on the administration of a particular IT system, which could be either UNIX, Windows, or both, versus an architect understands how all these applications and operating systems work, their interoperability, and their usefulness in the business for which they work. The architect title is seen as a graduation from many years of systems administration.

The graduation or change in titles from systems administrator to infrastructure architect will generally increase a systems administrator's base salary by about $20k–$40k or more. Usually the term architect is a promotion offered to top-notch systems administrators in an effort to retain them. No one knows better than a technology recruiter how titles affect the remuneration candidates can fetch just by adding or removing an additional word to or from their original titles.

Table 11.1 displays some of the job titles that project from the systems administrator position. These are examples of compensation increases that may occur as a result of title changes.

From:	To:	Salary Increase
Systems Administrator	Storage Architect	$20–30K
Network Administrator	Infrastructure Architect	$15–$25K
Database Engineer	Data Architect	$20–$30K

Table 11.1. Systems administration job roles.

No matter the title a company decides to give to their systems administrators or network engineers, the bottom line here is that the person with the title of an "architect" is a strategy thinker, commands more money, and sometimes doubles as a CIO; this person must have breadth and not necessarily depth of information and knowledge in technology and its alignment, integration, and adaptability in the organization.

Architect Roles in the House

There is a great disparity in how architects view their roles. They may all have the title "architect," but don't let the traditional knowledge of structural architecture sway you to think they are the same. Yes, they may be similar in that the architect, whether structural or technical, provides the overall design or big picture, but this loose definition is different depending on the organization and the goal it is trying to achieve.

Some architects may be involved in strategy formation, while others are involved in the day-to-day tasks of desktop and network administration and resource allocation. The four architect roles discussed in the following sections are Enterprise Architect, Solution Architect, Infrastructure Architect, and Storage Architect.

Enterprise Architect

The Enterprise Architect (EA) works on defining the architecture of the whole organization; the business, software, infrastructure, and security of the organization; and how these all work together in alignment with an organization's business direction.

A typical job description includes:
- o Establish a process that is focused on building and maintaining an enterprise and ensuring its alignment to the organization's business needs.
- o Understand business goals and create high-level design used and interpreted by network engineers, application designers, and database designers in an enterprise to manage information more effectively. This design must ensure the integration of all the parts of IT in an organization.
- o Facilitate the adaptation or change of technology to the changing business needs of an organization.

Required skills include a wide range of experience in different technologies and their interoperability, including:
- o Operating Systems: Sun Solaris, Windows Server, HP UNIX, Linux.
- o Database Systems: Oracle Server, SQL Server, Siebel, Teradata.
- o Development Tools: Java, C#, ASP.net, JavaScript; .NET, J2EE, EJB, Web Services, SOA, Design Patterns, AJAX, and many more.

Solution Architect

Previously known as the applications development manager, a Solution Architect's (SA) main role is to convert business requirements into a design that then forms the basis for a business solution. Through their design, the SA ensures that solutions meet the cost, schedule, scalability, availability, and requirements of the system.

A typical job description includes:

- o Understand business requirements and formulate designs, creating a solution structure that meets the various requirements.
- o Communicate the architecture; ensure that everyone involved in the design and implementation of the design understands the architecture.
- o Support the developers; mentor developers while ensuring that developers follow the overall architectural design.
- o Verify implementation of the design; ensure that the delivered system is consistent with the agreed architecture and meets requirements.

Required skills include a range of skills for creating blueprints and high-level design diagrams, such as UML (Unified Modeling Language), Database Design tools, Rational Rose Unified Process, and many more.

Infrastructure Architect

Previously known as Systems Administrator, Network Engineer, or IT Operations Manager, the Infrastructure Architect provides the architecture for any technology that is implemented for the whole organization, as opposed to technology for a specific business group. Typically he/she architects the infrastructure elements that every business group requires, such as networks, storage, operating systems, security, and messaging. The Infrastructure Architect also manages servers, middleware, and client systems.

A typical job description includes:

- o Develop and maintain the strategy, models, road maps, policies, and procedures for systems management and monitoring, security, capacity planning, storage, operating systems, servers, and networks.

Required skills include network configuration; storage management, performance, and scalability configuration; and security engineering.

Storage Architect

Now systems administrators are transitioning to another role, called Storage Architect—whether as a result of actual role/job function change or because the new name sounds more respectable. It is the enterprise administration of all data backup, archival, and recovery processes in an organization. Storage Architecture is becoming one of the most important aspects of infrastructure and network management. The cost of purchasing and managing storage has grown to be a significant part of any technology group as it relates to resources and staffing.

A typical job description includes:

- o Establish guidelines for space management, data backup, retrieval, and recovery.
- o Ensure the security and availability of stored data.
- o Purchase or negotiate contracts with off-site data storage companies.
- o Reduce total cost of ownership (TCO) through optimization.

Required skills include:

- o Backup and recovery solutions with EMC Networker, Symantec NetBackup, or IBM Tivoli Storage Manager (TSM).
- o Storage Area Network (SAN) storage consolidation and virtualization, backup to disk, virtual disk, tape, and virtual tape.
- o Experience with SAN technologies like Fiber Channel and IP-based storage network solutions.

Table 11.2 shows a breakdown of some of the requirements for the Storage Architect role. It also explains the reasons employers need the skills.

Requirements	Reasons
Subject matter expert in SAN (**S**torage **A**rea **N**etwork) technologies	The person in this role must understand the network infrastructure of shared storage, its makeup, interconnectivity, and how it is accessed.

An understanding of RAID (**R**edundant **A**rray of **I**ndependent **D**isks) technologies	RAID provides a way for storing the same data over multiple physical disks to ensure that if a hard disk fails, a redundant copy of the data can be accessed instead. The storage architect needs this knowledge in order to manage the availability of data.
Extensive understanding of Remote Replication (SRDF, SANCopy, MirrorView)	This skill is used for building disaster recovery solutions where data is stored or replicated to another site in order to achieve redundancy. This is a core skill requirement used for the creation of data recovery plans in organizations.
Backup, recovery, and disaster recovery (DR) schemes, schedules, and test plans	A key requirement skill for a storage architect. The architect is required to know how to back up and recover and also must be familiar with several vendor backup solutions.
Enterprise storage arrays, **G**iga**b**it **I**nterface **C**ontroller (GBIC)	A hot-swappable input/output device that plugs into a network port to link the port with the fiber optic network. The candidate must know of its existence, its flexibility, and the ability to connect an Ethernet network to a fiber optic one while the system is still on (hot-swap).
External SAN management software (**L**ogical **U**nit **N**umber (LUN) mapping, management)	SAN is the consolidation of storage resources into a single pool that minimizes administrative activities. The storage architect should be able to share the consolidated large storage device across many servers or applications. The sharing involves breaking the storage resources into chunks and assigning each chunk a logical unit number (LUN).
Fiber **C**hannel/**I**nternet **P**rotocol (FC/IP) or **I**nternet **S**mall **C**omputer **S**ystems **I**nterface (iSCSI) gateway and bridge devices	FC/IP is a high-speed interconnect protocol used in SANs to connect servers to shared storage. iSCSI is a protocol that enables transport of block data over IP networks. The storage architect needs to know how to configure these protocols in the organization's storage environment.

Just a **B**unch **O**f **D**isks (JBOD)	A group of disks housed in its own box. Knowledge in this and how it can be utilized in conjunction with other technologies is desired of the candidate.
NAS (**N**etwork **A**ttached **S**torage) appliance	A NAS is a server that runs an operating system designed for handling file systems that are accessible on a local area network through the TCP/IP protocol. The storage architect needs to know how to configure this on a network.

Table 11.2. Storage Architect job requirements.

Systems Administration Roles

The people in these roles implement and execute the design created by architects. Please note that in organizations where there are no architects, the systems administrators do both the high-level design (if able to) and the implementation. As mentioned before, the architect job comes with many years of experience performing systems administration duties in a myriad of systems. In this section we discuss two systems administrator roles—the Systems Engineer and the Security Engineer.

The Administrator versus Engineer

Before we delve into the two systems administrator roles, let's look at the perceived difference between the administrator and engineer titles and how it affects most systems administrator positions.

Before the proliferation of certifications from Microsoft, Sun, and Novell, the "engineer" title used to be given mostly to persons with a college degree in an engineering field. Though the engineer title (conferred through certifications to systems administrators) has now been watered down, you will find that it still wields some power, even if it's only in the form of increased compensation—and this may be its only intent. Employers recognize this as well, and some are taking a step to change the titles of their support staff from engineer to administrator.

The engineer is considered a more senior role than the administrator; the engineer is more involved in the design phase, while the administrator implements and supports the design. Whether a person is a network engineer or network administrator, their duties overlap each other.

Network Engineer

Depending on the organization, this is also referred to as Network Administrator. The Network Engineer's role is to design, plan, and configure complex routed local and wide area networks across an organization. This person configures network routers, switches, and firewalls; and is very familiar with all the network protocols and technologies, from TCP/IP, IPX/SPX, AppleTalk, SMB, IPSec, GRE and L2TP tunnels, VPN solutions, OSPF, RIP/RIP2, BGPv4, IPX RIP, to ISDN and frame relay. As a result of the myriad networks this individual designs, they are often seen with whiteboards, drawing interconnected network diagrams to visualize their design solutions. You will almost always find in their technical arsenal experience in centralized and automated network management software systems. This is one field where certification is always preferred; it may be because the process of certification in CISCO (the preferred network administration certification) and the like are a little more in depth than other certification tracks, thus making the individual with this certification more revered.

A typical job description includes:
- o The network engineer designs, plans, and implements the organization's network communications system.
- o Experienced with creating specifications for hardware and software selection.
- o Plans and designs the network infrastructure, bearing in mind capacity planning and budgeting guidelines.
- o Evaluates current network systems to propose and implement network system enhancements.
- o Tests, monitors, and tunes the network to ensure continuity and high availability of systems.
- o Maintains a continuous-learning state of mind in all areas of the organization's network, hardware, and software interoperability.

Required skills include:
- o Bachelor's degree and experience in local and wide area network design and implementation.
- o Minimum of eight years experience maintaining TCP/IP networks and configuring routers, switches, and firewalls.
- o Cisco Certified Network Associate (CCNA) and Cisco Certified Network Professional (CCNP) certifications may be required.

Table 11.3 contains common terms you find in resumes and job descriptions of Systems Administrators, with a focus on Network Engineering. Every Systems Administrator should be grounded in these terms and have hands-on experience configuring almost all of these in a network.

Term	Description
AppleTalk	A local area network protocol developed by Apple Computer.
ATM	Asynchronous Transfer Mode, a technology that can provide high-speed data transmission over either LANs or WANs.
BGPv4	Border Gateway Protocol, a protocol that allows routers to connect to each other.
Frame Relay	Network technology used for connecting devices on the Internet.
GRE	Generic Route Encapsulation, a method of encapsulating any network protocol in another protocol.
HSRP	Hot Standby Router Protocol, a Cisco routing protocol for fault-tolerant IP routing that enables a set of routers to work together.
IPSec	Internet Protocol Security, a VPN protocol for secure data exchange.
IPX/SPX	Internetwork Packet Exchange/Sequenced Packet Exchange, networking protocols used in Novell Netware networks.
ISDN	Integrated Services Digital Network, a wide area network data communication service provided by telephone companies. Used for high-speed dial-up connections to the Internet for the simultaneous delivery of audio, video, and data.
LDAP	Lightweight Directory Access Protocol, an Internet protocol that e-mail programs use to look up contact information or to locate organizations, individuals, and other resources, such as files and devices in a network.
OSPF	Open Shortest Path First, a routing protocol that determines the best path for routing IP traffic.

RIP/RIP2	Routing Information Protocol finds a route with the smallest number of hops between the source and destination.
SMDS	Switched Multimegabit Data Service is a high-speed WAN network communication service.
SMTP	Simple Mail Transfer Protocol is a text-based protocol used in messaging and e-mail.
SONET	Synchronous Optical Network defines how fiber-optic technology can deliver voice, data, and video over a network.
SSH	Secure Shell is a protocol or application used for securely connecting and executing commands on a remote computer.
TCP/IP	Transmission Control Protocol/Internet Protocol, a protocol used in the interconnection of computers on a network and Internet.

Table 11.3. Network terms in resumes and job descriptions.

Security Administrator

Keeping in mind that no computer system can ever be completely secure, the Security Administrator's main job is to make it difficult for intruders to compromise the operating system configuration. The Security Administrator develops security policies ensuring that only authorized users are permitted access to network resources and privileges. Using firewalls, encryption, audits, virus protection, and intrusion detection software, the Security Administrator ensures the secure operation of servers and network connections. As a result of security risks inherent in computing, security is now a basic requirement for any system administration position. But organizations are going a step further in creating specialized positions just for security, thus the Security Administrator.

A typical job description includes:
- o   Responsible for data security and network access.
- o   Implement Sarbanes Oxley access authorization requirements in organization.
- o   Comply with established access request control processes.
- o   Track and document the distribution of access requests and ports in network.

- o   Update and maintain antivirus software and virus definitions.
- o   Review audit logs and password compliances.
- o   Manage the application of security patches.
- o   Develop policies and procedures for security systems.

Required skills include:
- o   Seven to ten years of designing and implementing IT security processes.
- o   Experience configuring LAN/WAN, firewalls, proxy servers, IP protocols, DNS, DHCP, VPNs, and FTP security in Windows and/or UNIX environments.

Systems and Network Management Tools
Systems management applications and tools simplify the process of administering a network. Below are some tools that manage the operation, administration, and maintenance of network systems:
- o   Microsoft Operations Manager (MOM)
- o   Nagios Open Source Application
- o   IBM Tivoli NetView
- o   Hewlett-Packard HP OpenView
- o   CA Unicenter Network and Systems Management
- o   CiscoWorks LAN Management Solution

Application Systems Administration

Aside from network systems, business application systems also have their dedicated systems administrators. This is usually denoted with the name of the business application system preceding the systems administrator title; for example, for business applications like SQL Server, PeopleSoft, and Exchange, the titles for their administrators will be SQL Server Database Administrator, PeopleSoft Systems Administrator, and Exchange Systems Administrator.

The Application Systems Administrator is involved in the design, installation, and administration of the application server software. This person usually has in-depth knowledge and experience in every aspect of the application. The Application Systems Administrator performs optimization and performance tuning of the application. Another layer of authority is attained when this person receives a certification in the application they manage; this is often not a requirement, but causes employers to view candidates with more respect.

One of the greatest skills sets the Application Systems Administrator should have is problem solving and troubleshooting. With troubleshooting skills, the System Administrator frequently performs the role of third-level support persons, taking internal and external client calls that have been escalated from the first- and second-level support technicians.

Application Systems Administrators perform as both functional and technical administrators. Half of their time is spent performing functional duties that involve developing requirements for application enhancement, and the other half is spent performing administrative tasks, such as technical support, troubleshooting, and system maintenance.

Functional Responsibility of the Application Systems Administrator

The Application Systems Administrator contributes to the organization's long-term business process improvement projects. These processes involve interpreting user needs to develop requirements specifications, transforming these user needs into conceptual and physical designs, and implementing the designs in the business applications. Other functional tasks include:

- o Understanding and then modifying features of applications to suit the needs of the company.
- o Configuring applications integration with other modules or third-party applications.
- o Configuring applications security roles—different from the host system security roles. An example is where the security roles of a PeopleSoft application are configured differently from those of the operating system that hosts the application.
- o Developing and documenting operational procedures to ensure stability and availability of the applications.
- o Configuring system control settings to suit the environment.
- o Ensuring that applications flow conforms to government and accounting rules, controls, and compliance.
- o Helping in the formulation and creation of processes and procedures for training.

Technical Responsibility of the Application Systems Administrator

Another responsibility of the Application Systems Administrator is to provide overall deployment, support, management, and maintenance of the business applications, with tasks that include:

- o Performing daily monitoring of the applications server to maintain a highly available system.
- o Installing software patches, service packs, and updates on applications.
- o Troubleshooting applications server and end-user problems.
- o Working with vendors to resolve server applications issues.
- o Developing automation scripts for administering the applications.
- o Administering user accounts, file permissions, and print queues.
- o Performing system backups and full recovery disaster tests.
- o Carrying out system monitoring and performance tuning.

RESUME PHRASES   PeopleSoft Systems Administrator

Analysis, business process reengineering, fit-gap analysis, application designer, application engine, change assistant, component interface, Peopletools, SQR, process scheduler, object migrations, integration broker, PeopleCode, Analytic Server Framework, PeopleSoft Performance Monitor, application messaging, event notification, data mover.

Keywords of note: Integration broker, PeopleCode, SQR

Figure 11.1 Resume keywords for PeopleSoft Systems Administrator.

In Figure 11.1, we see a few of the common phrases that appear in the resume of a PeopleSoft Systems Administrator. You may notice a mixture of functional and technical skills. Aside from the phrases "analysis, business process reengineering. and fit-gap analysis," which are all functional skills, the rest are technical administration and development tool skills that a Systems Administrator is expected to be familiar with.

What We Learned

- Systems Administration includes the administration of networks and business applications software, referred to as Network Systems Administration and Application Systems Administration, respectively.
- Network Systems Management is the administration of enterprise-wide distributed computer systems, including hardware, software, their access, and the security of the network.
- Network Systems Administrators now represent not only network administration, but a newer and high-level systems administration, referred to as Infrastructure Architecture.
- The Infrastructure Architect is a well-rounded person who is grounded in the business as well as technical aspects of the organization.
- The architect title is given to individuals depending on the organization and the goal the organization is trying to achieve. There isn't a standard requirement for the makeup of an architect from one organization to the other. Some architects may be involved in strategy formation, while others are involved in the day-to-day tasks of network administration.
- Architects of note are the Enterprise Architect, Solution Architect, Infrastructure Architect, and Storage Architect.
  o The Enterprise Architect works on the architecture of the whole organization.
  o The Solution Architect converts business requirements into a design, which then forms the basis for a business solution.
  o The Infrastructure Architect provides the architecture for any technology that is implemented for the whole organization.
  o The Storage Architect manages the enterprise administration of data access, backup, archival, and recovery processes in an organization.
- Systems Administrator roles include the Network Engineer and Security Engineer. These are the people who implement and execute the design created by the architects.
  o The Network Engineer can also be referred to as the Network Administrator. This person's role is to design, plan, and configure complex local and wide area networks across an organization.

o The Security Engineer makes it difficult for intruders to compromise the operating system security configuration.

- Application Systems Administration is the management of business applications. PeopleSoft Systems Administrator and Exchange Systems Administrator are examples of Application Systems Administrators. The Application Systems Administrator is involved in the design, installation, and administration of the applications server. This person usually has in-depth knowledge and experience in every aspect of the applications.

Chapter 12

SAP Enterprise Resource Planning (ERP) Overview

In This Chapter

- What is ERP?
- SAP business software
- SAP ERP Business Solutions

In this chapter you will see an overview of SAP business applications, especially the Enterprise Resource Planning (ERP). The different modules of the ERP software will be described, and you will also see the skills requirements for each module. The word "module" was used in the past to separate each category of the SAP business software, but now the term used is "solutions"—SAP Business Solutions. In this chapter we will also review the resume and job description of one of the most sought-after SAP job roles, Financial and Management Accounting, FI/CO.

What Is ERP?

Enterprise Resource Planning, in the simplest terms, refers to the integration of software applications used for operations, finance, administration, planning, and purchasing for the internal and external business process of an organization. The largest supplier of this type of software is the company SAP, AG., maker of not only the ERP software but many other business suites.

SAP, AG. is a German software company that started in 1972. The acronym SAP means Systems, Applications, and Products. The SAP system is a modular application that covers all aspects of business operations, such as finance, human resource administration, production planning, sales, and distribution, to name a few. These modules can exist and perform independent of each other, but the true benefit of using SAP comes when the solutions or modules are implemented as an integrated system. With the SAP software, companies are able to manage many aspects of their business processes in one place. SAP develops business applications for major industry sectors, such as the following:

o   Service industries
o   Financial services
o   Process industries
o   Discrete industries
o   Consumer industries
o   Public services

Evolution of SAP ERP Application

The SAP evolution started when five former IBM employees in Germany decided to form a company to develop real-time business application software. Their first software, SAP R/1, was launched in 1973; in 1979, the R/2 ERP application was released for mainframe computers; and in 1992, the R/3 client/server software system was introduced. The R stands for real-time data processing.

Current ERP versions are SAP R/3 Enterprise Release 4.70, SAP R/3 Release 4.6C, SAP R/3 Release 4.6B, SAP R/3 Release 4.5B, and SAP R/3 Release 4.0B. The R/3 releases have upgrade paths to the most recent release, which is the ERP Central Component (ECC) 2005. Figure 12.1 shows how SAP has evolved over the years since inception.

Figure 12.1. SAP ERP evolution.

SAP Business Software

SAP's software is built for complete application integration, but this does not mean that the applications cannot function independently. SAP customers can pick and choose the individual application suite they want to run. When run individually, each application suite targets the business processes. Collectively, they form an integrated business application suite. Currently, all SAP business applications run on SAP NetWeaver, which is a platform that supports software created with Service Oriented Architecture (SOA).

The following are included in SAP's Business Software:
- o   SAP Customer Relationship Management (CRM)
- o   SAP Enterprise Resource Planning (ERP)
- o   SAP Product Life Cycle Management (PLM)
- o   SAP Supply Chain Management (SCM)
- o   SAP Supplier Relationship Management (SRM)
- o   SAP Human Capital Management (HCM)
- o   SAP Business Intelligence (BI)
- o   SAP Financial Supply Chain Management (FSCM)

SAP ERP Overview

SAP ERP offers solutions that support all business operation facets, from accounting and human resources to product development and sales. Key software functions in SAP ERP include analytics, financials, human capital management, procurement and logistics, product development and manufacturing, sales and service, and corporate services. Figure 12.2 illustrates all the components and subcomponents of the ERP system functionality.

ERP Functionality	Subcomponents				
Analytics	Financial Analytics	Operations Analytics	Workforce Analytics		
Financials	Financial Supply Chain Management	Financial Accounting	Management Accounting	Corporate Governance	
Human Capital Management	Talent Management	Workforce Management	Workforce Development		
Procurement and Logistics	Procurement	Inventory & Warehouse Management	Logistics	Transportation Management	
Product Development & Manufacturing	Production Planning	Manufacturing	Product Development	Data Management	
Sales & Service	Sales & Orders	Aftermarket Sales & Service	Professional Services		
Corporate Services	Real Estate Management	Asset Management	Travel Management	Env., Health & Safety	Quality Management

Figure 12.2. SAP ERP map.

Analytics

SAP ERP provides analytic software that helps companies analyze their business, develop plans and budgets, and track performance. SAP ERP Analytics supports Financial, Operations, and Workforce analysis and reporting. Figure 12.3 depicts the subcomponents of the Analytics functionality.

Analytics	Financial Analytics	Operations Analytics	Workforce Analytics

Figure 12.3. SAP Analytics.

Financial Analytics

Using the financial analytics tools, organizations are able to report on overhead costs allocation, manage costs incurred by products and services, and analyze the profitability of products and services. The skills requirements for the SAP Financial Analytics Consultant include:

- o Ability to implement financial and accounting analysis for financial planning and control
- o Ability to work with business owners to define and analyze reporting requirements
- o Experience in SAP ERP Central Component (ECC), SAP NetWeaver, and Business Warehouse (BW)
- o Understanding of business processes in Financial Accounting, such as General Ledger and Accounts Payable and Receivable
- o Experience in performing the following analyses:
  - Financial and Management Reporting
  - Financial Planning, Budgeting, and Forecasting
  - Profitability Analytics
  - Product and Service Cost Analytics
  - Overhead Cost Analytics
  - Working Capital and Cash Flow Management
- • Ability to use report painter, drilldown reporting for the evaluation of financial data Financials—General Ledger, Financials—Account Payables/Account Receivables (FI-GL, FI-AP/AR)
- • Experience in the development of queries and reports from SAP BI/BW environment using SAP tools such as Query Designer, Business Explorer (BEx), and Web Application Designer

Operations Analytics

This system provides preconfigured applications for budget and forecast planning. It's also used for building operations reports. The skills requirements for the SAP Operations Analytics Consultant include:

- o Experience with SAP ECC, SAP R/3 Enterprise, and SAP BW
- o Experience in SAP ERP Operations Analytics, including features and functions that support these business activities:
  - Sales Planning
  - Procurement Analytics
  - Inventory and Warehouse Management Analytics
  - Manufacturing Analytics
  - Transportation Analytics
  - Sales Analytics
  - Customer Service Analytics
  - Program and Project Management Analytics

- Quality Management Analytics
- Asset Analytics and Performance Optimization

Workforce Analytics

About six hundred preconfigured Human Capital Management (HCM) reports are predefined in SAP ERP. This makes it fairly easy for consultants to immediately run these reports and learn about workforce issues and opportunities within their organizations. The skills requirements for the SAP Workforce Analytics Consultant include:

- o Knowledge of the SAP-HR functional modules listed below:
  - HR/Personnel Administration
  - Benefits Management
  - Time Management
  - Organization Management
  - Manager and Employee Self-Serve
- o Experience with ERP Central Component (ECC), SAP Business Warehouse, and Intelligence BW/BI
- o Experience at identifying early-stage trends, predicting human-capital investment demands, and tracking workforce costs and the ROI associated with HR projects
- o Experience in SAP Human Capital Management reporting and analysis solutions, including:
  - Workforce Planning
  - Workforce Cost Planning and Simulation
  - Workforce Benchmarking
  - Workforce Process Analytics and Measurement
  - Talent Management Analytics and Measurement
  - Strategic Alignment
- o Experience in building queries with Ad Hoc Query and SAP Query
- o Experience integrating HCM in the Business Information Warehouse and Strategic Enterprise Management
- o Linking the results of workforce analysis directly to headcount planning, budgeting, recruiting, and learning.

Financials

SAP Financials includes the functionality of core accounting and reporting capabilities with financial supply chain, treasury, compliance, and performance management. This solution comes with applications such as Financial Supply Chain Management (FSCM), Financial Accounting (FI), Management Accounting (CO), and Corporate Governance. Figure 12.4 depicts the subcomponents of the Financials functionality.

Financials	Financial Supply Chain Management	Financial Accounting	Management Accounting	Corporate Governance

Figure 12.4. ERP Financials.

SAP Financial Supply Chain Management (SAP FSCM)

SAP FSCM includes applications such as treasury and risk management, in-house cash, credit management, electronic invoicing and payments, dispute management, and collections management. These applications provide an integrated solution for managing electronic customer billing, accounts receivables, collections, customer credit, and handling of billing disputes. Skills requirements for the SAP FSCM Consultant consist of:

o   Experience in ERP Central Component (ECC)
o   Experience with FSCM applications such as Biller Direct, Collection Management, Dispute Management, and Credit Management
o   Experience in SAP R/3 FI-AR (Accounts Receivable)
o   Hands-on project experience with some FSCM modules, including:
  ▪ Cash and Liquidity Management
  ▪ Debit/Credit Interest Processing
  ▪ Transaction Charges and Interest Penalty
  ▪ Dispatch Expenses
  ▪ Cash Evaluation and Condition Measures
  ▪ Payment Planning and Processing
  ▪ Cash Concentration Planned and Actual Execution
  ▪ Account Balancing Act and Tracking
  ▪ Bank Statement Processing, including reconciliation and clearing
  ▪ Notification Processing
  ▪ End-of-Day Cash Forecasting, Planning, and Reporting
  ▪ Investments Processing, Analyzing Accounting, and Reporting

Financial Accounting (FI)

The Financial Accounting module includes applications that help organizations perform functions in general ledger, accounts receivable, accounts payable, SAP contract accounts, asset accounting, bank accounting, cash journal, accounting, inventory accounting, tax accounting, accrual accounting, fast close, and financial statements. Skills requirements for the FI Consultant consist of:

- o A background in finance is a highly desirable requirement for someone in this field. This is because the candidate will have a good understanding of all aspects of the accounting process, from accounts receivables and payables and revenue recognition to the financial close process.
- o Hands-on project experience with the development cycle, from business process definition and configuration to training, support, and fixes
- o Configuration skills in SAP ERP Central Component FI (AP, AR, GL, and Fixed Assets)

SAP Management Accounting (CO)

The Management Accounting module includes profit center accounting, cost center and internal order accounting, investment management, product cost accounting (including project accounting), profitability accounting, and activity-based costing. Usually the CO-controlling skill goes hand-in-hand with FI (Financial Accounting); however, when these skills are separated in a job description, this is a good indication that near-perfect skills in either of the areas is highly desirable. Skills requirements for the CO Consultant include:

- o Experience in ECC 6.0
- o Experience in CO-PA (Profitability Analysis) and CO-PC (Product Costing)
- o Experience in Cost Center Accounting, Cost Center Allocations, and Profit Center Accounting
- o Experience in Costing-Based Profitability Analysis and Material Ledger

Corporate Governance

Corporate Governance software includes solutions for governance, risk, and compliance (GRC). These solutions are used to promote and achieve compliance, governance, and risk mitigation. Skills requirements for the GRC Consultant include:

o Experience in Automated General Computer Control (GCC) collection

o Experience in IT Governance and Information Security Control Frameworks, such as Control Objectives for Information and related Technology (CoBiT), Information Technology Infrastructure Library (ITIL), and International Organization for Standardization (ISO) 27001

o Experience in standards, process, and tools associated with ERM (Enterprise Risk Management), Information Risk Management, and Information Security Architecture

o Experience in IT Risks evaluation and compliances that affect the security of systems, networks, telecommunication, applications, and databases in a global multiplatform business environment

Human Capital Management

SAP ERP HCM is a software suite for talent management processes. It includes all human resource processes, such as employee administration, payroll, and legal reporting, and supports compliance with regulations. The human capital management functions are available as extensions to Microsoft Office through software called Duet. Duet is SAP's software collaboration with Microsoft; it enables access to SAP business processes and data through Microsoft Office applications. The HCM software suite includes applications such as Talent Management, Workforce Management, and Workforce Development. Figure 12.5 depicts the subcomponents of the Human Capital Management functionality.

Human Capital Management	Talent Management	Workforce Management	Workforce Development

Figure 12.5. ERP Human Capital Management.

Talent Management

The SAP Talent Management includes the following functions: recruitment, succession management, enterprise learning management, employee performance management, and compensation management. The Talent Management module is used in finding the best people, developing their talent, and retaining top performers. Skills requirements for the Talent Management Consultant include:

o   Knowledge in SAP HCM business processes
o   Knowledge in SAP ERP Central Component
o   Experience with any (or all) of the following:
   ▪   SAP e-Recruiting
   ▪   Personnel Management
   ▪   Succession Management
   ▪   Enterprise Learning Management
   ▪   Employee Performance Management
   ▪   Compensation Management
   ▪   SAP Employee Self Service(ESS)/Manager Self
       Service (MSS)
   ▪   Experience with HR system integration with FI/
       CO or any other modules

Workforce Management (WFM)

WFM in SAP ERP HCM supports workforce process management, including employee administration, organizational management, global employee management, benefits management, time and attendance, payroll, and legal reporting. Skills requirements for the WFM Consultant include:

o   Experience with SAP HR 4.6 C, ECC 6.0
o   Workforce Management processes in the areas of Forecasting, Time & Attendance, Talent Management, Human Resources Analytics, Budgeting, Leave, and Work Flow

Procurement and Logistics

Procurement and Logistics is used for reducing operating costs in inventory and warehouse management. Figure 12.6 depicts the subcomponents of the Procurement and Logistics Execution functionality.

Procurement and Logistics	Procurement	Inventory & Warehouse Management	Logistics	Transportation Management

Figure 12.6. Procurement and Logistics.

Procurement

Procurement in SAP ERP includes requisitioning, purchase request processing, trading contract management, purchase order processing, receiving, financial settlement, managing catalog content, compliance management, supplier collaboration, and commodity management. Skills requirements for the SAP Procurement Management Consultant include:

- o Experience with ERP ECC 6.0
- o Ability to implement the procurement functions of SAP ERP and SAP Supply Chain Management
- o Experience with Quality Management (QM), distribution, warehousing, and planning
- o Experience with SAP R/3 functionality in Materials Management (MM)
- o Other function experiences include:
  - Implementation of specific business processes: configuration and mapping of the company structure, master data, and business processes in the SAP system
  - Customizing settings in materials management
  - Customizing settings for purchasing, inventory management, physical inventory, account determination, and organizational levels
  - Entering goods movements in the SAP system and performing relevant implementations for special functions
  - Preparing and performing a physical inventory of warehouse stock
  - Goods receipts, goods issues, and transfer posting
  - Planning and performing a physical inventory

Inventory and Warehouse Management

Inventory Management includes planning, entry, and documentation of stock movements like goods receipts, stocktaking, and stock transfers. Warehouse Management process involves storage of materials, crossdocking, warehousing, and physical stocktaking. Skills requirements for the SAP Inventory and Warehouse Management Consultant include:

- o Business background in Warehouse Management, Distribution, or Transportation
- o SAP R/3 configuration skills in the area of Logistics
- o Knowledge in TMS (Transportation Management System)
- o Knowledge in Warehouse Management Systems (WMS)
- o Knowledge in Materials Management/Purchasing, Inventory Management, and Warehouse Management
- o Knowledge in RF Bar Code Integration

o Extended Warehouse Management (EWM)
o All the above experiences in an SAP R/3, 4.7 environment and/or in an ECC 6.0 platform

Logistics

Logistics in the procurement and logistics module includes the inbound and outbound processes involved in movement of goods from their manufacturers to customers. Inbound includes all the processes that occur when goods are received in the warehouse from their manufacturers. Inbound process has the capability to manage the receipt of goods and handle advanced shipping notifications. Outbound covers the activities for the shipping of customers' goods to their destination. Some outbound processes include monitoring delivery activities and documenting proof of delivery. Skills requirements for the SAP Logistics Execution Consultant include:

o Knowledge in all aspects of Logistics Execution (LES) and Transportation
o Experience in Warehouse Management (WM) and full life cycle SAP WM implementations, migration, and implementation support
o Experience converting business requirements into technical designs
o Functional experience in Goods Receipt and Goods Issue processes in Inventory Management (IM) and WM, SAP MM Inventory Management, SAP Warehouse Management, SAP Shipping, and SAP Transportation
o Experience integrating IM, WM, Materials Management (MM), and Transportation modules with other modules such as Production Planning (PP) and Sales and Distribution (SD)
o Experience maintaining and enhancing SAP Shipping and Transportation Modules

Transportation

SAP ERP covers transportation execution that provides a solution to create, execute, and monitor shipments. Some transportation execution processes are also included in SAP Supply Chain Management (SCM) and consist of transportation execution and freight costing. Skills requirements for the SAP Transportation Management Consultant include:

- o Understanding of SAP Order Fulfillment Processes with Order to Cash (OTC)
- o Hands-on SAP Sales and Distribution (SD), shipping, and transportation functionality experience
- o Understanding of Planned Shipments and Shipment to Carriers Assignment
- o Integration of SAP Supply Chain Management (SCM) to Transportation Planning in SAP ERP
- o Understanding of Freight Management in the areas of Transportation Requests Capture, Dynamic Route Determination, Credit Limit Check, Send Confirmation, and Distance Determination Service
- o Understanding of Planning and Dispatching in the areas of Load Consolidation, Mode and Route Optimization, Transportation Service Provider Selection, Transportation Visibility, and Shipping
- o Understanding of Rating, Billing, and Settlement in the areas of Supplier Transportation Charges, Customer Transportation Charges, Transportation Charge Rates, and Integrate Invoice Request

Product Development and Manufacturing

The SAP software has modules or solutions that facilitate the process of bringing ideas from inception to market, with solutions covering Production Planning, Manufacturing, Product Development, and Data Management. Figure 12.7 depicts the subcomponents of the Product Development and Manufacturing functionality.

Product Development & Manufacturing	Production Planning	Manufacturing	Product Development	Data Management

Figure 12.7. ERP Product Development and Manufacturing.

Production Planning

The software supports a range of strategies for production planning and execution. With this software, organizations can plan and schedule factory production. Skills requirements for the SAP Production Planning Consultant include:

- o Hands-on configuration experience with SAP Production Planning
- o Full life-cycle implementations, including project preparation, requirements gathering and analysis, Go-Live, postproduction support, and end-user documentation and training
- o Experience in the utilization and configuration of several Production Planning (PP) functionalities, which may include the following abilities:
  - To perform Material Requirements Planning (MRP)
  - To evaluate MRP results/MRP lists
  - To perform interactive planning of planned orders
  - To convert planned orders into production orders
  - To convert planned orders into purchase requisitions
  - To perform interactive planning of purchase requisitions
- o Knowledge of SAP PLM Asset Life-Cycle Management and Plant Maintenance
- o Knowledge of SAP SCM Manufacturing and Advanced Planning
- o Ability to integrate Production Planning (PP) with other SAP modules

Manufacturing Execution

This software module provides visibility and transparency across production and manufacturing processes. Skills requirements for the SAP Manufacturing Consultant include:

- o Functional knowledge of SAP R/3, ECC6.0, Production Planning(PP), PI, Quality Management (QM), and Manufacturing, either the Process Industry or Discrete Industry functionality
- o Hands-on experience in troubleshooting Production Support Related Issues in Logistics Area, Materials Management, Inventory Management, Warehouse Management, Sales and Distribution (MM/IM/WM/SD)

o Experience with Product Planning, Manufacturing Execution, Inventory/Warehouse Management, Bar Coding, Product Costing, and Quality Management

o Electronic batch record for continuously documenting the production process (meets FDA/GMP regulations)

o Knowledge in PP processes, including BOM (Bill of Materials), Forecasting, Recipes, Work Centers, Routings, MRP, and Reporting

o Experience in integration of SAP MM with other associated modules

o Experience in the configuration of SAP Manufacturing business process in ERP and SCM, which may include the following:
   - Schedule order and confirm order
   - Material handling
   - Batch management and serial number assignment
   - Release and print order
   - Generate inspection lots
   - Document management
   - External processing
   - Report order progress
   - Backorder processing
   - Rework and costs management
   - Shop floor information system

Product Development

This software module involves product definition, requirements gathering, product development, supplier sourcing, and the integration of people and information in the New Product Development and Introduction (NPDI) process. Skills requirements for the SAP Product Development Consultant include:

o Production development functionality experience with either the process industry or discrete industry

o Experience in the configuration of SAP Product Development business process in ERP, which may include the following:
   - Set up initial recipe
   - Calculate product properties in Specification Management
   - Define product trials and tests with Trials Management
   - Execute product trials
   - Request new ingredients and packaging

- Create new ingredients and packaging on request
- Request ingredients and packaging information from vendor
- Calculate product properties
- Approve ingredient and packaging specifications

Lifecycle Data Management

This module deals with the centralization of document, change, and configuration management from product definition and invention to production. Skills requirements for the SAP Life Cycle Data Management Consultant include:

o Experience with the integration of Life Cycle Data Management with other ERP business processes

o Experience with NetWeaver Business Intelligence (BI), CAD Integration, SAP ERP Central Component 6.0, and SAP PLM 7.0

o Knowledge of SAP Easy Document Management and cProjects

o Experience with the document management system and its process flow, including:

- Creating a document,
- Securing and storing files,
- Document approval,
- Document conversion,
- Document use and view process, and
- Document distribution

o Experience with the Specification Management process for use with Raw Materials or Recipes specifications; the process flow may require knowledge in the following areas:

- Editing specification,
- Editing phrases,
- Determinations of secondary data,
- Evaluations of specification,
- Editing report templates,
- Editing generated reports, and
- Report evaluation

o Experience with the Change and Configuration Management process, including the following processes:

- Create change notification,
- Process change notification,
- Create engineering change request (or change master record),
- Process and release engineering change,

- Process order changes, and
- Manage product configuration
o Knowledge of the business process supported by Variant Configuration and Classification System
o Product Structure Browser and Engineering Workbench

Sales and Services

The sales and services module facilitates the management of the sales department. Used for the management of sales activities, tasks, contacts, and customers, it is also used to manage the sales process from customer request and quotation to order and invoice. Figure 12.8 depicts the subcomponents of the Sales and Services functionality.

Sales & Services	Sales & Orders	Aftermarket Sales & Service	Professional Services

Figure12.8. ERP Sales and Services.

Sales and Orders

Sales Order Management in SAP ERP ECC 6.0 includes creating and processing sales orders, sales document types, item categories, partner determination, and contracts and scheduling agreements. Skills requirements for the SAP Sales and Orders Consultant include:
o SAP Sales and Distribution functional knowledge
o SAP ERP includes the following Sales Order Management functions:
  - E-commerce
  - Quotation and Order Management
  - Contract Management and Pricing
  - Billing.
  - Sales Portals
  - Inbound Telesales
  - Sales Analytics and Planning
o Other technical skills required for the Sales and Distribution (SD) Consultant are :
  - Managing Auctions
  - Inquiry Processing
  - Quotation Processing
  - Trading Contract Management
  - Sales Order Processing (Sales Orders)
  - Incentive and Commission Management

- Returnable Packaging Management
- Consignment Stock Processing

Aftermarket Sales and Services

In this area, SAP has software solutions and/or modules that help manufacturers target the Aftermarket Sales and Services market segment. The functions in this area include processes for:

o Service Contract Management: This module gives its users the visibility to manage contract details like warranty expirations, compliance, and service level agreements.

o Customer Service and Support: In this module, there is a full integration of full call-center applications, knowledge databases for problem resolution and cross- and upselling opportunities, and call history and warranty information in order to simplify the customer service process.

o Other modules or solutions under the Aftermarket Sales and Services are warranty and claims management, service part management, and installed base management.

Skills requirements for the SAP Sales and Services Consultant, usually for Project Managers, include:

o SAP R/3 experience of ECC version 5.0 or higher

o Service Sales and Service Contract Management

o Customer Service and Support with integration with some of the following modules:

- *PM Structuring Technical Systems* for information on structuring and managing technical objects
- *FI-AA Asset Accounting MM—Services Management* for information on service records
- *PM—Maintenance Notifications* for information on maintenance notification functionality
- *PM—Maintenance Orders* for information on maintenance order functionality
- *SD—Sales, Sales Order Processing* for information on managing and billing sales orders and service contracts
- *PS—Project System* for information on using projects

o Installed Base Management as part of the Plant Maintenance (PM) and Customer Service (CS) application components

o Warranty and Claims Management integration with master data management (MM, SD, CS, PM) and pricing (SD), posting FI documents (FI/CO), and evaluation of the warranty data (SAP BW)

o Help desk processing, which includes creating, processing, configuration of notification types, and completing service notifications

o Returns and repairs processing, which includes repair order processing and returns delivery, repair processing, delivery, and billing

o Field service planning, which includes processing of service orders, configuring order types, scheduling and capacity planning, materials planning, and completion confirmation

Professional Services

Professional service delivery covers the structured tracking of all activities, recording time spent on all project services, and analyzing profitability for each project. This includes the management of the following processes: project planning and scoping, resource and time management, quotation processing, sales order processing, managing employee time and attendance, travel expense management, project accounting, and billing. The skills requirements for the SAP Professional Services Delivery Consultant include:

o Experience in SAP Service Delivery Management

o Experience in running SAP operations in a business environment

o SAP functional knowledge in Manufacturing, Supply Chain Management, Sales and Distribution, and Finance

o Knowledge of SAP support processes and tools such as Solution Manager

o Experience in creating and managing Service Level Agreements

o Ability to communicate SAP objectives, performance, and key metrics within the organization

o Strong people management and negotiation skills

Corporate Services

With the SAP ERP Corporate Services solution, organizations can manage real estate, enterprise assets, project portfolios, corporate travel, environment, health and safety compliance, and global trade services more effectively. Figure 12.9 depicts the subcomponents of the Corporate Services functionality.

Corporate Services	Real Estate Management	Asset Management	Travel Management	Env., Health & Safety	Quality Management

Figure 12.9. Corporate Services.

In Real Estate Management, SAP ERP Corporate Services supports the administration of commercial and residential real estate. The Enterprise Asset Management solution supports asset maintenance, maintenance cost budgeting, and maintenance execution.

Travel Management

This component is integrated with SAP ERP Financials and SAP ERP Human Capital Management (SAP ERP HCM) solutions; the SAP Travel Management controls all phases of travel management, including submitting initial requests, planning, online booking, and submitting and settling travel expenses. Skills requirements for the SAP Travel Management Consultant include:

- o Hands-on configuration experience with SAP ECC6 SAP Travel Management
- o Experience with configuring the work flow for Travel Management application component to support approval procedures
- o Experience in analyzing travel planning processes and policies and implementing a solution that increases compliance with the policies. This solution should include:
  - Travel planning
  - Travel requests
  - Reimbursement of expenses after a business trip
- o Experience with SAP HR, FI, AP, Credit Card, and Currency Conversion
- o Experience with Credit Card functions and international currency exchange rates
- o Experience with SAP FI Accounts Payable Module

Environment, Health, and Safety Compliance Management

This component is used for the management of product safety; hazardous substances, waste, and emissions management; product compliance;

industrial hygiene; safety programs; and occupational health programs. Skills requirements for the SAP EHS Consultant include:

- o Experience in the implementation and configuration of ERP 6.0 versions
- o Experienced in the integration of EHS functionalities with SAP ERP
- o Experience with the EH&S module that includes Industrial Health/Safety and hazardous waste management
- o Experience in the configuration of some of the following processes:
  - EH&S IHS Accident Management
  - EH&S OH Health Surveillance Protocol
  - Emissions Management with SAP Environmental Compliance
  - Environment, Health, and Safety Compliance Management Map
  - Environmental Auditing When Purchasing Hazardous Materials
  - Environmental Vendor Managed Inventory
  - Hazardous Substance Management for Customer Tailored Products
  - Integrated Dangerous Goods Check in Sales and Shipping
  - Originator-Related Costs Assignment of Waste Generation

Quality Management

SAP ERP Corporate Services Quality Management (QM) supports total quality management, inspection planning and processing, prevention, and continuous process improvement. Skills requirements for the SAP QM Consultant include:

- o Experience with SAP ECC 6.0 Quality Management (QM)
- o A good understanding of the QM functionalities
- o Experienced with the integration of QM functionalities with other SAP ERP business components
- o Experience supporting phases of a SAP QM implementation, including:
  - Project preparation
  - Requirements gathering and analysis
  - Business blueprint
  - Go-Live and postproduction support

- End-user documentation and training

o Experience with SAP QM submodules

SAP Candidate Resume

Using one of the most sought-after SAP module positions, SAP FI/CO, we will review a job description to illustrate what a SAP resume looks like, what to look for, and how to review a resume for a FI/CO position.

The one thing that is immediately obvious with resumes of SAP consultants is the length. It's usually about eight, twelve, or more pages long, with very many three-to-six-month contracts at various client sites. Longer resumes tell you that the owner was a traveling consultant; shorter resumes usually belong to full-time candidates with less implementation cycles and experience. See Figure 12.10 for a sample resume.

SAMPLE

SAP FI/CO Consultant

Summary
Andy is a FI/CO 4.6C consultant with ten years experience in SAP implementation. Areas of expertise include design and configuration of the following FI/CO modules: GL, AP, AR, FA, Banking, Treasury, Corporate Finance Management, Cost Center Accounting, Profit Center Accounting, and COPA. Additional experiences in SAP include MM, Purchasing, and Sales & Distribution module integration.

Professional Experience
ABC Consulting   January 2006–Present
- Completed five full life-cycle implementations
- Configured and implemented FICO (GL, AR, AP, and CCA) and integration configuration between FI-AA, MM, SD, and PM
- Implemented FI-AP, FI-AA, and FI-GL modules for AR & Credit
- Performed information gathering, interface design, data conversion and mapping to configure GL, AR, AP, CCA, PCA, and COPA
- Tested and provided production support for upgrade project from 4.7 to ECC 5.0

> ■ Performed required integration between FI/CO, MM, and SD modules

Figure 12.10. Sample SAP FI/CO resume.

Resume Focus Points

Differentiators that may qualify one candidate over the others include industry experience, number of implementations, understanding of functional process, and module integration.

Industry Expertise: Very important is the prior experience a candidate has working in the employer's industry. SAP FI/CO experience in Pharmaceuticals may be different from that in Oil and Gas.

Implementations: How many projects has this candidate implemented? A candidate with more implementations under his or her belt is more attractive to a hiring manager. Multiple implementations are indicative of a person's experience, which demonstrates that the candidate has worked through more issues than a candidate that has worked for the same company for ten years but experienced less than two implementations. On the other hand, measuring a candidate's experience solely by the number of projects completed could at times be misleading without looking at whether those projects were *full life-cycle* implementations. A blueprint project involving specifications and design only (without actual implementation) that lasted six months will reflect a different experience from an upgrade project that ran from blueprint to go-live (actual implementation).

Understanding of the Module and Process: How well a candidate understands the functionality of the module and whether they have functional experience can be a major differentiator. This factor is accentuated whenever you see the phrase "*accounting background a major plus*" in a job description for the finance and accounting module FI/CO. The phrase indicates that candidates with accounting and finance background are a better fit than candidates with only IT background. These candidates will understand the application functionalities and processes better than a person with any other background.

Experience with Integration: A company may start off implementing just one SAP module, but may decide to purchase another module down the road where the second module needs to integrate with the first. In seeking a candidate for this position, this company would prefer a person with experience integrating modules together. This is where a candidate with consulting experience may win the day. Traveling consultants with experience in many projects have greater exposure to different module integration.

SAP FI/CO Alphabet Soup

Acronyms with no explanations can be a major annoyance and turn off recruiters from further studying resumes and job descriptions. Table 12.1 lists the meanings of the FI/CO terms in Andy's resume.

Alphabet	Meaning
FI/CO	Financial/Management Accounting and Controlling
GL	General Ledger
AP	Accounts Payables
AR	Accounts Receivables
FA	Fixed Assets
COPA	Controlling Profitability Analysis
MM	Materials Management
SD	Sales & Distribution
ECC	ERP Central Component
FI-AA	Asset Accounting
PM	Plant Maintenance
PCA	Profit Center Accounting
CO-CCA	Cost Center Accounting
CO-OPA	Orders/Projects
FM	Funds Management
S-AM	Account Management
FS-AM-IM	Item Management
EC-CS	Consolidation
FI-CA	Contract Accounts
CO-PC	Product Cost Controlling

Table 12.1. SAP FI/CO terms.

You can see from Figure 12.10 that Andy scored points in many of the important requirements for SAP consultants. He has completed five life-cycle implementations, which is two more than the average requirement in job descriptions, which indicates that Andy may have had some experience consulting at various client sites. He's also involved in almost all the phases of implementation—information gathering, interface design, data conversion and mapping, testing, and production support.

He's also performed integration between the main module FI/CO and other modules: Materials Management (MM) and Sales and Distribution (SD) modules. Two missing points in Andy's resume are any industry experience/focus and any stated understanding of the module's functionalities.

SAP FI/CO Job Description

When you study any job description, there are always key skills that you pay close attention to. As you identify them, mark or underline these, as they will form the must-haves for the job role. Following the guidelines in Anatomy of a Technical Job Requisition found in Chapter 1 of this book, you may want to find out more about this job description from the hiring manager. Depending on your experience in recruiting for a particular job role, reviewing a job description for a position you've recruited for several times before may become an automatic process for you. This is because you now know all the requirements by heart, especially if the position is for an established client or a chosen industry vertical, such as legal, medical, hospitality, or government.

Looking at the SAP FI/CO job description in Figure 12.11, you will notice that the must-haves have been identified with the underline format; these are the points that will be further analyzed.

SAMPLE

Overview
Provide functional and implementation support as a FI/CO configuration specialist in these SAP R/3 modules: FI-Finance (GL, SPL, FM, AP, AR), CO Controlling.

Responsibilities
- Very knowledgeable with required SAP product module business processes, configuration requirements, and integration with other modules.
- Responsible for requirements analysis, configuration, testing, problem solving, user interface, and overall application support for SAP FI/CO.

- Perform all tasks in the development cycle from business process definition, configuration, testing, problem solving, and follow-up, to co-coordinating transports to production, performing training, and postlive support.
- Heavily involved in FMS (Financial Management Systems) Product Development (PD) throughout the roll-out development cycle.
- Designing, developing, implementing, and controlling FICO module areas using templates to meet global and local legal/business requirements ensuring all core FMS business requirements are maintained, new business needs are proactively supported, and new SAP functionality delivers business benefits.

Requirements
- Five years of SAP FI/CO configuration experience.
- Should have integration experience with at least three other SAP modules.
- Understanding of integration points between the FICO and PS/SD/MM Modules.
- Three prior life-cycle SAP implementations as a FI /CO consultant.
- Key strengths in the GL, Fixed Assets, AP, AR, and Special Ledger submodules.
- Experience working on ECC 6.0 is a plus.
- CPA or equivalent accounting qualification is preferred.

Figure 12.11. Sample SAP FI/CO job description.

Responsibilities and Requirements Analysis

Analyzing the responsibilities and requirements identified in Figure 12.11, we look at the underlined points. Most of these points have been discussed in the previous section (SAP Candidate Resume), where topics like experience with integration, industry expertise, and number of implementations are seen as major points in a candidate's resume. Further explanation of these important points follows.

o Integration with other modules: The hiring manager is looking for a person with experience integrating one module with many others. The FI/CO module cannot work on its own in an ERP environment; it needs to be tied to the organization's other business processes, such as materials management (MM) or sales and distribution (SD).

o Responsible for requirements analysis, configuration, testing, problem solving, user interface, and overall application support for SAP FI/CO: The job description here is looking for a person that knows all the phases of the implementation process from beginning to end, where the candidate has performed all tasks in the implementation cycle.

o Three prior life-cycle SAP implementations: A candidate with three or more implementations under their belt is a seasoned consultant and attractive to the hiring manager.

o CPA or equivalent accounting qualification preferred: FI/CO is financial and accounting management and controlling. A person with real-life functional experience, such as a CPA (Certified Public Accountant), possesses hands-on practical work experience of how the finance and accounting process works and is very attractive to the hiring manager.

Suitability

You can see from Figures 12.10 and 12.11 that Andy scored points in many of the important requirements for SAP consultants. He has completed five life-cycle implementations, which is two more than the average requirement in job descriptions, which indicates that Andy may have had some experience consulting at various client sites. He's also involved in almost all the phases of implementation—information gathering, interface design, data conversion and mapping, testing, and production support.

He's also performed integration between the main module FI/CO and other modules: Materials Management (MM) and Sales and Distribution (SD) modules. Two missing points in Andy's resume are any industry experience/focus and any stated understanding of the modules' functionalities.

What We Learned

- Enterprise Resource Planning is the integration of software applications used for operations, finance, administration, planning, and purchasing for the internal and external business process of an organization. The largest supplier of this type of software is the company SAP, maker of not only the ERP software but many other business suites.

- SAP develops business applications for major industry sectors, such as Service Industries, Financial Services, Process Industries, Discrete Industries, Consumer Industries, and Public Services.

- SAP's software is built for complete application integration, but this does not mean that they cannot function individually. SAP customers can pick and choose the individual application suite they want to run. When run individually, each application suite targets the business processes. Collectively, they form a tightly integrated business application suite. The following are SAP's Business Software: SAP Customer Relationship Management (CRM), SAP Enterprise Resource Planning (ERP), SAP Product Life Cycle Management (PLM), SAP Supply Chain Management (SCM), and SAP Supplier Relationship Management (SRM).

- Analytics: SAP ERP provides analytic software that helps companies analyze their business, develop plans and budgets, and track performance.

- SAP Financials includes the functionality of core accounting and reporting capabilities with financial supply chain, treasury, compliance, and performance management. This solution comes with applications such as Financial Supply Chain Management (FSCM), Financial Accounting (FI), Management Accounting (CO), and Corporate Governance.

- SAP ERP HCM is a software suite for talent management processes. It includes all human resource processes, such as employee administration, payroll, and legal reporting, and supports compliance with regulations. Human Capital Management functions are available as extensions to Microsoft Office through software called Duet.

- SAP Talent Management includes the following functions: recruitment, succession management, enterprise learning management, employee performance management, and compensation management. The Talent Management module is used in finding the best people, developing their talent, and retaining top performers.

- Procurement and Logistics Execution is used for reducing operating costs in inventory and warehouse management.

- Procurement in SAP ERP includes: Requisitioning, Purchase Request Processing, Trading Contract Management, Purchase Order Processing, Receiving, Financial Settlement, Managing Catalog Content, Compliance Management, Supplier Collaboration, and Commodity Management.

- The SAP software has modules or solutions that facilitate the process of bringing ideas from inception to market, with solutions including Production Planning, Manufacturing, Product Development, and Data Management.

- The Sales and Services module facilitates the management of the sales department. Used for the management of sales activities, tasks, contacts, and customers, it is also used to manage the sales process from customer request and quotation to order and invoice.

- With the SAP ERP Corporate Services solution, organizations can manage real estate, enterprise assets, project portfolios, corporate travel, environment, health and safety compliance, and global trade services more effectively.

Chapter 13

Certifications

In This Chapter

- The value of certification
- The cheating game
- The question about certification
- Development team certifications
- Business team certifications
- System and network administration certifications

Software Certifications Inc. defines certification as a means to define the common body of knowledge for a particular practice. It evaluates an individual's ability to apply that knowledge to practice. Acquiring certification in any field indicates a professional level of competence in the principles and practices associated with that profession.

Certification does not guarantee that a candidate is an expert in a field but shows that the candidate has the potential to be good at that particular field. It demonstrates the candidate's ability to learn and experience new heights.

In this chapter we review the certification requirements of organizations, answering the "why do you need a certified candidate?" question. This chapter also reveals the certification requirements for operating systems, programming software, database, business analysis, and project management.

The Value of Certification

Though one school of thought claims that certification was created by vendors as a means to popularize their products, the vendors argue that certification increases the value and the earning power of the candidate. This may have been true a decade ago when the craze was on for certifications such as MCSE (Microsoft Certified Systems Engineer) and CCNA (Cisco Certified Network Associate); hiring companies wanted to prove they had the best skilled people working for them, and the candidates wanted the prestige accorded to a certified individual.

Nowadays it is unclear who gets the most value from certifications. Is it the vendor, whose name appears as a prefix on the titles of hundreds of thousands of individuals, thereby creating an increased awareness for the vendor's products? Or is it the candidate who is looking for a boost in their career and thinks that certification will do just that? Does it really matter? Both parties seem to be gaining something; it's a win-win for all, even though one party (the bigger guy) may be getting more out of it than the other.

The value of IT certification has been watered down over the years following its crazed beginnings in the 1990s. When the craze began, it was assumed that individuals were required to go through classroom training programs in order to take the associated test. The training classes added real value to the program because individuals sat together in a classroom and actually learned how to install, configure, and troubleshoot applications.

This was the case for a long time until self-study books hit the shelves and people knew that they could study and take the test without attending an expensive training class; the result increased the number of certified candidates at an alarming rate. The natural effect of the proliferation of certified individuals in the industry was that the value of certifications started diminishing.

There are at least two other reasons why the value of certification started going downhill. Cheating by test takers is one, and the hiring organization's preference for experience over certification is the other.

The Cheating Game

There is an inherent need for humans to seek to find an easier way to accomplish a given task. For certification, it started with *Braindumps,* an Internet site where test takers dumped subsets of the questions and answers they encountered during their tests. These subsets grew in size and sophistication until the dumps included the complete exact fifty questions and answers for each exam title.

The dump sites were easily accessible by anyone with Internet access who had an interest to cheat. Test scores increasingly started hitting 100 percent for most vendor-sponsored exams, with more people becoming certified as product administrators who knew little about the products they were hired to administer, and as a result became a nuisance to the vendors.

The product vendors started seeking ways to shut down the dump sites. One of the ways was to require test takers to sign a nondisclosure agreement that outlined the possibility of decertification if they were found to have used any of the cheat sites. The other way was to seek the prosecution of the brain dump site owners. The proliferation of the brain dumps slowed down after this, but the information is still available today and sometimes sold as test preparation guides.

The cheating created a bad reputation for certified individuals. The ones that actually studied and passed their exams were especially infuriated with the cheat sheets and dumps. Today there are Web sites that act as anti-braindump police, who monitor and advise on which sites seem to be cheat sites versus the honest test preparation Web sites.

As you can understand, this has led to the devaluation of certifications in the IT industry as a whole, much to the chagrin of the honestly certified individuals.

Experience over Certification

A good question to ask your hiring manager is this: "*If presented with two candidates, one certified and the other not, which would you choose if both seem to have the required experience?*" The hiring manager may not tell you this, but whatever answer you get may depend on 1) if the hiring manager has been certified at one time or the other, 2) his or her perceived value for certifications in general, and 3) the level of expertise needed for the job—high- or low-level skills.

For the more technically inclined positions like systems administration and desktop support, certification may be a good factor for hiring a person. If the position requires business as well as technical skills (usually found in technical project managers or business analysts), certification may be of less value to the hiring manager. This is because the skills sets for technical project managers and business analysts are more business related, and thus can sometimes truly be achieved through experience and not tests and certifications.

Depending on the perceived value of certification to the hiring manager, experience may be preferable over certification.

The Question About Certification

"Why certification?" is a twofold question: Why does a candidate need to certify, and why does an employer need a certified individual?

In answer to the former question, one of the reasons candidates get certified in the IT industry is to call more attention to themselves and their skills, letting potential employers know that they possess the required competency in the skill in question. The follow-up question may then be: *"Does a candidate need certification to prove she is able to perform?"* The answers are yes, no, and it depends.

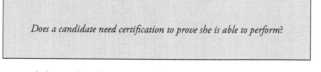

Does a candidate need certification to prove she is able to perform?

Yes for candidates that have something to prove (usually candidates with one to three years of experience in the desired field); yes for candidates that are able to take the time to improve on their skills; yes for candidates that are looking for advancement, who want the chance to prove they can do it as well as the next person and that they have an aptitude for learning and growing.

On the other hand, there are some very skilled workers that do not need a piece of paper to prove they can deliver on the job. These are usually candidates that have several years experience in their specified field and do not have the time nor patience for certifications.

Why does an employer need a certified individual? As a technical recruiter with a certification requirement listed in a job requisition, you must seek to understand the reasoning behind this requirement. Some of the reasons employers may require certification are:

- o The employer is in an industry that requires certified employees in order to maintain their license to practice.
- o The employer may have identified "certification" as a good trait in current employees and want to ensure they follow the same success measures in future employees.
- o The employer may be a vendor partner and, as such, may have a vendor partnership requirement to employ a number of certified individuals.

These are just a few reasons, but the job is yours to find out exactly why the hiring manager requires a certified individual when a noncertified but experienced person could suffice.

Profile of the Certified versus Noncertificd

There are many qualified candidates available with the experience needed but without the certification. These same candidates will hardly seek certifications unless they are out of work or in between jobs.

Figure 13.1. Profile of a Noncertified candidate (NCC).

The profile of a noncertified candidate, as illustrated in Figure 13.1, shows that 1) this person has worked for the same company for more than five years and is not looking to change organizations; 2) this person has more than ten years experience in a particular field; 3) he scorns the certification process; 4) she immediately dislikes organizations that require certification over experience; and 5) this person, when faced with interviewing a certified candidate, will be the toughest interviewer to please. As an interviewer, this noncertified experienced person wants to ensure that the candidate has more knowledge in the brain than what's presented on the resume.

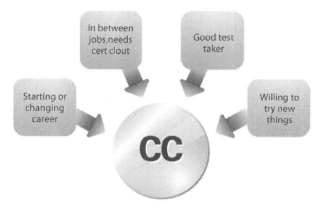

Figure 13.2. Profile of a Certified Candidate (CC).

A look at Figure 13.2 illustrates that the certified candidate may be 1) starting or changing careers, 2) in between jobs and needing the added clout of a certification, 3) a good test taker, 4) more willing to try new things.

Product and Business Process Certifications

In this section we will review certifications for vendor products and business processes, such as software development, database, operating system, business analysis, and project management certifications.

Application Development Certifications

Application development in this section refers to the work of individuals involved in writing application code. We will review certifications from vendors like Microsoft and Java.

Microsoft

According to Microsoft, there are three development tracks for application developers: the Microsoft Certified Professional Developer (MCPD), Microsoft Certified Application Developer (MCAD), and Microsoft Certified Solution Developer (MCSD). Though these certifications are mostly based on the use of the same development tools, the main differentiator between them lies in the type of applications developed, which can include Windows-based, enterprise class, and Web-based applications. Details of these three certifications follow.

- o *Microsoft Certified Professional Developer (MCPD)*: This certification requires two to three years of experience developing solutions using Visual Studio and the Microsoft .NET Framework. With the MCPD certification, developers can build interactive, data-driven ASP.NET applications for intranet and Internet uses, or choose to focus on building enterprise distributed solutions that focus on ASP.NET and Windows Forms.
- o *Microsoft Certified Application Developer (MCAD)*: This certification requires one or two years of experience in building and maintaining applications. The MCAD certification equips individuals with the skills to develop and maintain department-level applications, Web/desktop clients, and back-end data services.
- o *Microsoft Certified Solution Developer (MCSD)*: Persons with this certification usually have two or more years of experience developing and maintaining applications. The MCSD certification makes it possible for the individual to design and develop business solutions.

Java

From Sun Microsystems, the Java development track goes from first becoming a Sun Certified Associate, moving on up to becoming a Sun Certified Programmer, and then afterward progressing to an advanced specialized certification that can help propel candidates into specific job roles. Details of these three certifications follow.

o *Sun Certified Java Associate (SCJA)*: Sun Microsystems training and certification online documentation refers to this as an ideal entry into application development using Java technologies. It validates basic knowledge of object-oriented concepts and the Java programming language, as well as general knowledge of Java platforms and technologies.

o *Sun Certified Java Programmer (SCJP)*: This is the next level up the Sun development ladder, as noted from Sun's certification and training online documentation. It's for programmers interested in demonstrating proficiency in the fundamentals of the Java programming language.

o *Sun Certified Java Developer (SCJD)*: This certification is intended for developers who want to demonstrate advanced proficiency in the Java programming language using the Java SE (Standard Edition). Requirements for this certification include a completed programming assignment from the candidate, an essay exam, and certification as a Sun Certified Programmer (SCJP).

Database Certifications

In this section we review the certifications from Microsoft and Oracle for database administration (DBA) and development (DBE) tracks.

Microsoft

For SQL Server, it started with the Microsoft Certified Database Administrator (MCDBA) certification, which helped candidates demonstrate their ability to design, implement, and administer Microsoft SQL Server databases. This certification tested for the combination of skills in database administration as well as database development. Please note that this certification is primarily for Microsoft SQL Server 7.0 and 2000 versions.

The new generation certification is the Microsoft Certified Information Technology Professional (MCITP). With this certification Microsoft is categorizing skills based on job roles. The job roles for Microsoft SQL Server are the MCITP: Database Administrator, MCITP: Database Developer, and the MCITP: Business Intelligence Developer. The distinctions among these follow.

o *MCITP: Database Administrator*: This job role certification requires two exams: 1) Microsoft SQL Server implementation and maintenance, and 2) designing, optimizing, and maintaining a database administrative solution using Microsoft SQL Server.

o *MCITP: Database Developer*: This job role certification requires two exams: 1) database development, and 2) designing database solutions and data access using Microsoft SQL Server.

o *MCITP: Business Intelligence Developer*: Two exams are required: 1) Microsoft SQL Server Business Intelligence—Development and Maintenance, and 2) designing a business intelligence solution by using Microsoft SQL Server.

Oracle

A little different from the other vendors, which merely *suggest* that candidates attend training, Oracle *requires* that candidates attend classroom training before they can be certified on most of their technologies. This requirement can be expensive for the individual but almost always guarantees the individual has proven knowledge of the product. The following certifications are available from Oracle:

o *Oracle Database 11g - Administrator Certified Associate*: Candidates are required to pass two exams (no training requirement).

o *Oracle Database 11g - Administrator Certified Professional*: Requires one training from Oracle + one exam + hands-on course requirement form (this is a form submitted to Oracle that verifies that the candidate attended an approved hands-on course).

o *Oracle Database 11g - Administrator Certified Master*: Requires two trainings from Oracle + one exam + hands-on course requirement form.

o *Oracle Database 11g - Performance Tuning*: Requires prior certification as a Certified Professional + one training from Oracle + one exam + hands-on course requirement form.

o *Oracle Database 11g - SQL Certified Expert*: One exam is required. There is no training requirement.

Software Testing

There are two main software certification organizations: the International Software Testing Qualification Board (ISTQB) and the Quality Assurance Institute (QAI). Each of these organizations has certification qualification requirements that share similar values with the other organization. In the following sections, we review each organization's software testing certifications.

International Software Testing Qualification Board (ISTQB)

This organization created a standard for software testers that are in the beginning stages as well as advanced-level candidates, with the Foundation Level and Advanced Level Certified Tester certifications, respectively.

o *Certified Tester, Foundation Level (CTFL)*: According to the American Software Testing Qualifications Board, the Foundation Level certification is aimed at anyone involved in software testing. This includes people in roles such as testers, test analysts, test engineers, test consultants, test managers, and user acceptance testers. The Foundation Level certification requires no prior experience or certifications.

o *Certified Tester, Advanced Level (CTAL)*: According to the American Software Testing Qualifications Board, the Advanced Level certification is aimed at testers who have at least three years experience in software testing. This includes people in roles such as testers, test analysts, test engineers, test consultants, test managers, and user acceptance testers. Requirements for this certification include Foundation Level certification and three years of verifiable full-time experience in software testing, development, or quality assurance.

Quality Assurance Institute (QAI)

QAI began software certifications in 1980, and like ISTQB, QAI's software testing certification starts at the foundation level. Following are details of its various certifications:

o *Certified Associate in Software Testing (CAST)*: As noted on the QAI's Web site, the CAST is the foundation-level certification for software testers, software developers, system analysts, and fresh engineering graduates. Certified individuals are able to demonstrate an understanding of testing principles and practices.

o *Certified Software Tester (CSTE)*: This certification is a practitioner-level certification for individuals with a number of years of experience as test engineers, test architects, design analysts, and test leads.

o *Certified Manager of Software Testing (CMST)*: This certification is for managerial-level individuals and is suitable for test managers, test leads, architects, and project managers. Certified individuals are able to demonstrate their competence to practice and manage the software testing function.

Business Process Certifications

Certifications under the business process categories have more stringent eligibility requirements than their technology counterparts, probably because the organizations that govern these certifications are not trying to sell any products and so can afford to make the entry rules as difficult as possible, allowing only the determined to pursue and attain these certifications. We look at the business analysis and project management certifications.

Business Analysis

In this section we will introduce two business analysis certification organizations: the Quality Assurance Institute (QAI) and the International Institute of Business Analysis (IIBA).

- o *Certified Software Business Analyst (CSBA)*: From QAI's certification information, this is a practitioner-level certification for business analysts, project leads, and architects who are currently working. Attaining this certification demonstrates proficiency to manage the link between business and information technology communities. The prerequisites to qualify for this certification include a four-year degree from college or six years experience in an information technology field and currently working or having worked at any time within the prior eighteen months in business analysis. After the prerequisites are validated, the candidate is approved to take the certification exam.

- o *Certified Business Analysis Professional (CBAP)*: From IIBA certification information, the minimum prerequisites for this certification include five years of work experience, demonstrated business analysis work experience and expertise for a minimum of six months, high school or equivalent education, twenty-one hours of professional development in the last four years, and two references from a career manager, client (internal or external), or another CBAP. After the prerequisites are validated, the candidate is approved to take the certification exam.

Project Management

The Project Management Institute (PMI) offers a number of certifications that test the ability of candidates to manage projects and apply standards during project delivery. Like the business analysis certification, the requirements for project management certification are not as easy as what is found in technical certification. The more popular project management certifications are the Project Management Professional (PMP) and Program Management Professional (PgMP).

> o *Project Management Professional (PMP)*: From the PMI certification information, the PMP certification demonstrates knowledge and skill in leading and directing project teams and in delivering project results within the constraints of schedule, budget, and resources. Prerequisites require that only those who lead and direct teams to deliver projects within the constraints of schedule, budget, and scope are to apply to take the test; in addition, applicants are required to have a bachelor's degree, three to five years of project management experience, and thirty-five hours of project management education.

> o *Program Management Professional (PgMP)*: The PMI certification information also notes that PgMP certification recognizes experience and skill in overseeing multiple, related projects that are aligned within an organizational strategy. Only those who manage program activities that span functions, organizations, geographic regions, and cultures can apply. Requirements vary for bachelor's degree and high school diploma holders, but include four years of project management experience and four to seven years of program management experience.

Operating System Certifications

Operating systems can either be network or desktop based. In this section we review certifications from Microsoft, Sun, and Red Hat Linux.

Microsoft Certified Systems Administrator/Microsoft Certified Systems Engineer (MCSA/MCSE):

The MCSE certification was introduced in the 1990s; the MCSA track was introduced shortly after. Both the MCSE and MCSA ensure that certificate holders are able to:

  o   Manage and maintain a Microsoft Windows Server 2003/2008 Environment.
  o   Implement, manage, and maintain a Microsoft Windows Server 2003/2008 Network Infrastructure.
  o   Install, configure, and administer and support Windows XP, Vista, and Windows 7 Professional.

Table 13.1 illustrates the differences and similarities between the MCSA and MCSE job roles.

	MCSE (Systems Engineer)	MCSA (Systems Administrator)
Responsibilities	Plan, design, and implement Microsoft Windows server solutions and architectures in medium- to large-size companies	Implement, manage, and maintain the typically complex computing environment of medium- to large-size companies
Prior Experience	Have at least one year of experience implementing and administering network operating systems and desktop operating systems.	Have six to twelve months of experience administering client and network operating systems.
Job Titles	Systems engineer, network engineer, systems analyst, network analyst, or technical consultant.	Systems administrator, network administrator, information systems administrator, network operations analyst, network technician, or technical support specialist

Table 13.1. Comparison between MCSA Systems Administrator and MCSE Systems Engineer.

The MCSE and MCSA certifications can be received on older as well as on newer versions of the Windows operating systems.

Sun Certified Systems Administrator (SCSA)

This is for systems administrators tasked with performing systems administration on the Solaris Operating System. This certification ensures that certificate holders are able to:

- o   Manage file systems and install software.
- o   Perform system boot and shutdown procedures.
- o   Perform user and security administration.
- o   Manage network printers and system processes.
- o   Perform system backups and restore.
- o   Manage virtual file systems and core dumps.
- o   Manage storage volumes, control access, and configure system messaging.

Sun Certified Network Administrator (SCNA)

This is for the experienced systems administrators responsible for administering Sun systems in a local area network. Criteria for certification include extensive knowledge on Solaris network administration, including how to configure and manage the network interface layer, the network (Transport layers in the OSI Model), network applications, and the Solaris IP Filter.

Sun Certified Security Administrator (SCSECA)

This certification is for systems administrators who have previous experience administering security in a Solaris Operating System. You may find that candidates that have this certification are already certified as either a Sun Certified Systems Administrator (SCSA) and/or a Sun Certified Network Administrator (SCNA). Criteria for this certification include the following:

- o   In-depth knowledge of UNIX and Solaris O/S features.
- o   Extensive knowledge of Solaris O/S security administration features.
- o   Experience in user account and password security, network security, auditing, and zone security.

Red Hat Certified Engineer (RHCE)

This certification ensures that certificate holders are able to:

o   Install and configure Red Hat Linux and understand limitations of hardware.

o   Configure basic networking and file systems for a network.

o   Configure the X Window System and perform essential Red Hat Linux systems administration, including configuring basic security for a network server.

o   Set up and manage common enterprise networking (IP) services for the organization.

What We Learned

- Certification is a means to define the common body of knowledge for a particular practice, evaluating an individual's ability to apply that knowledge to practice.

- Certification may have been created by vendors as a means to garner more awareness for their products, but it is also an avenue for candidates to increase their earning power.

- Certification has been devalued by cheating by test takers and by the hiring company's value for experience over certification.

- The noncertified candidate has typically worked for the same company for more than five years, is not looking to change organizations, and has more than ten years experience in a particular field; while the certified candidate may be starting or changing careers or be in between jobs and needing the added clout of certification.

- Product and business process certifications include software development, database, operating system, business analysis, and project management.

Bibliography

AG, S. (2001). *Help: SAP Corporation.* Retrieved August 13, 2009, from SAP Web site: http://www.sap.com.

American Software Testing Qualifications Board. (n.d.). *Software Testing Certification.* Retrieved September 30, 2009, from ASTQB Web site: http://www.astqb.org/.

Beginners Co. (n.d.). *Visual Basic 6 Application Development Part 2.* Retrieved July 10, 2009, from Beginners.co.uk Web site: http://tutorials. beginners.co.uk/visual-basic-6-application-development-part-2-distributed-applications.htm#.

Booch, G., R. A. Maksimchuk, M. W. Engle, B. J. Young, J. Conallen, and K. A. Houston. (2007). *Object-Oriented Analysis and Design with Applications.* Upper Saddle River, NJ. Pearson Education, Inc.

Brooks, F. (1987). *Software Requirements.* No Silver Bullet: Essence and Accidents of Software Engineering. IEEE Computer Society Press, 10–19.

Cockerell, P. (1987). *ARM Assembly Language Programming: 1987.* Retrieved January 21, 2009, from http://www.peter-cockerell.net/aalp/.

Computer Technology Documentation Project. (n.d.). *Repeaters, Bridges, Routers, and Gateways.* Retrieved November 24, 2008, from The Computer Technology Documentation Project Web site: http://www.comptechdoc.org/independent/networking/guide/netdevices.html.

Discovery Communications. (n.d.). *How Stuff Works-Operating Systems.* Retrieved August 10, 2008, from How Stuff Works Web site: computer.howstuffworks.com.

Habraken, J., and M. Hayden. (2004). *Teach Yourself Networking in 24 Hours.* Indianapolis, IN. Sams Publishing.

Hoffer, J., George, J., and Valacichi, J. (2002). *Modern Systems Analysis and Design* 5th Edition. Upper Saddle River, NJ. Prentice Hall.

IBM Corporation. (n.d.). *IBM Academic Initiative: An Introduction to the Mainframe: Large Scale Commercial Computing.* Retrieved September 20, 2009, from IBM corporate Web site: http://www-03.ibm.com/systems/z/advantages/charter/skills_coursematerials.html#LargeScaleCC.

247

Information Management and SourceMedia, Inc. (n.d.). *Glossary*. Retrieved November 29, 2008, from Information Management Web site: www.dmreview.com/glossary/d.html.

Johnston, A. (n.d.). *The Role of the Agile Architect*. Retrieved September 4, 2009, from http://www.agilearchitect.org/agile/role.htm.

Kendall, K., and J. Kendall. *Systems Analysis and Design*. Englewood, NJ. Prentice Hall.

Kettner, John, Mike Ebbers, Wayne O'Brien, and Bill Ogden. (August 2009). *Introduction to the New Mainframe: z/OS Basics*. Retrieved September 5, 2009, from Oracle Corporate Web site: www.redbooks.ibm.com/abstracts/sg246366.html?Open. IBM RedBooks.

Knowledge Rush. (n.d.). *Acorn RISC Machine*. Retrieved December 12, 2008, from Knowledge Rush Web site: http://www.knowledgerush.com/kr/encyclopedia/Acorn_RISC_Machine/.

Markiewicz, M. E., and C. J. Lucena. (2001). *Object Oriented Framework Development* Retrieved June 15, 2009, from Association of Computer Machinery Web site: http://www.acm.org/crossroads/xrds7-4/frameworks.html.

Microsoft Corporation. (n.d.). *Microsoft Learning: Microsoft Certifications by Name*. Retrieved August 23, 2009, from Microsoft Web site: http://www.microsoft.com/learning/en/us/certification/view-by-name.aspx.

Microsoft Corporation. (n.d.). *Training*. Retrieved June 24, 2008, from Microsoft Corporation Web site: www.microsoft.com/training.

Microsoft Developers Network. (2007, December). *The Infrastructure Landscape: A Matter of Perspective*. Retrieved November 11, 2008, from Microsoft Corporation MSDN Architect Center Web site: http://msdn.microsoft.com/en-us/library/bb896739.aspx.

Microsoft Press. (1998). *Networking Essentials: MCSE Self-Paced Kit (Microsoft Training Product)*. Redmond, WA: Microsoft Press.

Norton, M. J. (2001, January 1). *Networking as a 2nd Language*. Retrieved from O'Reilly Web site: http://www.oreillynet.com/pub/ct/23.

Oracle Press. (n.d.). *Oracle® Database VLDB and Partitioning Guide*. Retrieved April 12, 2009, from Oracle Corporate Web site: http://download.oracle.com/docs/cd/B28359_01/server.111/b32024/part_admin.htm.

Patton, R. (2006). *Software Testing*. Indianapolis, IN: Sams Publishing.

Pendse, Nigel. (n.d.). *The OLAP Report*. Retrieved February 9, 2009, from Business Application Research Center Web site: http://www.olapreport.com/glossary.htm.

Platt, M. (n.d.). *Architecture Type Definitions*. Retrieved November 12, 2008, from Michael Platt Weblog: Blogs.technet.com/michael_platt/archive/2005/10/07/412167.aspx.

Procedural programming. (2009, August 13). *Wikipedia, The Free Encyclopedia*. Retrieved August 13, 2009, from http://en.wikipedia.org/w/index.php?title=Procedural_programming&oldid=307715937.

Project Management Institute (PMI). (n.d.). *About PMI's Credentials*. Retrieved October 1, 2009, from PMI Web site: http://www.pmi.org/CareerDevelopment/Pages/AboutPMIsCredentials.aspx.

Quality Assurance Institute. (n.d.). *Software Testing Certification*. Retrieved October 1, 2009, from QAI Global Institute Web site: http://www.qaiglobalinstitute.com/innerpages/Default.asp.

Red Hat. (n.d.). *Red Hat Certification*. Retrieved January 29, 2009, from Red Hat Web site: http://www.redhat.com/training/.

Rozanski, N., and E. Woods. (2005). *Software Systems Architecture: Working With Stakeholders Using Viewpoints and Perspectives*. Upper Saddle River, NJ: Pearson Education.

SAP. (2009). *History: SAP AG Company*. Retrieved April 2, 2009, from SAP Web site: http://www.sap.com.

Software Certifications Inc. (n.d.). *Certified Software Business Analyst (CSBA)*. Retrieved October 1, 2009, from Software Certifications Web site: http://www.softwarecertifications.org/qai_csba.htm.

Sommerville, I. A. (1997). *Viewpoints: Principles, problems and a practical approach to requirements engineering*. Annals of Software Engineering, Volume 3, Pages 101-130.

Steinke, S. (2000). *Network Tutorial: A Complete Introduction to Networks*. San Francisco: CMP Books.

Sun Microsystems. (n.d.). *Java Certification*. Retrieved September 30, 2009, from Sun Microsystems Web site: http://www.sun.com/training/certification/java/index.xml.

University of Albany. (n.d.). *Glossary*. Retrieved August 10, 2008, from University of Albany Web site: www.albany.edu/its/glossary.htm.

University of California, Irvine. (n.d.). *Enterprise Architect Role*. Retrieved from University of California Web site: http://apps.adcom.uci.edu/EnterpriseArch/EARole.html.

VPN Tools. (n.d.). Networking Tools, Retrieved January 29, 2009 from www.vpntools.com.

Wang, W. (2008). *Beginning Programming for Dummies*. Indianapolis, IN: Wiley Publishing, Inc.

Wiegers, K. (1999). *Software Requirements*. Redmond, WA: Microsoft Press.

Wikipedia. (n.d.). Networking – LAN,WAN, Retrieved August 19, 2009, from www.wikipedia.org.

Wreski, D. (1998, August 22). *Linux Security Administrator's Guide v0.98.* Retrieved September 10, 2009, from http://www.nic.com/~dave/ SecurityAdminGuide/SecurityAdminGuide.html.

Glossary

Active Directory (AD)
The directory service stores information about objects on a network and makes this information available to users and network administrators. Active Directory gives network users access to permitted resources anywhere on the network using a single log-on process.

Address Resolution Protocol (ARP)
Address Resolution Protocol maps hardware address to IP address for delivery of data on a local area network.

AppleTalk
A local area network protocol developed by Apple Computer.

Asynchronous Transfer Mode (ATM)
Asynchronous Transfer Mode is a technology that can provide high-speed data transmission over LANs or WANs.

Border Gateway Protocol version 4 (BGPv4)
Border Gateway Protocol allows routers to connect to each other.

Configuration Management
This is a process of tracking different development builds/versions of the software for revision, change, and release control.

Domain
A domain is a group of computers that are part of a network and share a common directory database. A domain is administered as a unit with common rules and procedures.

Domain Name System (DNS)
DNS is a database system that translates an IP address into a hostname that is easy to remember. For example, converting an IP like 209.121.191.98 to kensington.com.

Dynamic Host Configuration Protocol (DHCP)
DHCP is a TCP/IP service protocol that dynamically leases IP addresses to eligible network client computers.

Frame Relay
Frame relay is a network technology used for connecting devices on the Internet.

FreeBSD
FreeBSD is a flavor of UNIX operating system; it's free and originally from Berkeley Software Distribution (BSD).

Generic Route Encapsulation (GRE)
Generic Route Encapsulation is a method of encapsulating any network protocol in another protocol.

Hot Standby Router Protocol (HSRP)
Hot Standby Router Protocol is a Cisco routing protocol for fault-tolerant IP routing that enables a set of routers to work together.

Hypertext Transfer Protocol (HTTP/HTTPS)
In the OSI model, the Hypertext Transfer Protocol is located in the application layer and is used for linking files, text, graphics, etc. between browsers and other applications on the Internet.

Integrated Services Digital Network (ISDN)
Integrated Services Digital Network is a wide area network data communication service provided by telephone companies. Used for high-speed dial-up connections to the Internet for the delivery of data, audio, and video.

Internet Information Server (IIS)
IIS is a software service that supports Web site creation, configuration, and management, along with other Internet functions.

Internet Message Access Protocol (IMAP)
Internet Message Access Protocol is an Internet protocol used for e-mail retrieval.

Internet Protocol Security (IPSec)
Internet Protocol Security is a protocol that secures IP communications with encryption, data authentication, and confidentiality.

Internet Protocol version 6 (IPv6)

IPv6 is a newer Internet Protocol version that expands the address length of 32 bits up to 128 bits.

Internetwork Packet Exchange/Sequenced Packet Exchange (IPX/SPX)

Internetwork Packet Exchange/Sequenced Packet Exchange is a network protocol used by Novell Netware.

Lightweight Directory Access Protocol (LDAP)

LDAP is a protocol for querying and accessing information directories—such as organizations, individuals, phone numbers, and addresses—and other resources, such as files and devices in a network.

Listserv

Listserv is an electronic mailing list software used by people to communicate with other members that are subscribed to the list.

Local Area Network (LAN)

A Local Area Network is a computer network covering a small geographic area, like a home, or one location, such as an office or school.

MhonArc

Based on Perl programming language, MhonArc is a free e-mail archiving program that converts mails to HTML.

Network File System (NFS)

This is a UNIX-based protocol that allows computers access to files over a network.

Network Information Systems and Yellow Pages (NIS/YP)

NIS/YP is used in the UNIX environment and operates similar to Windows DHCP, allowing computers within a domain to share common network addressing configurations.

Open Shortest Path First (OSPF)

Open Shortest Path First is a routing protocol that determines the best path for routing IP traffic.

Point-to-Point Protocol (PPP)

Point-to-Point Protocol provides dial-up networked connection to networks. PPP is commonly used by Internet Service Providers (ISPs) as the dial-up protocol for connecting customers to their networks.

Post Office Protocol Version 3 (POP3)
Located in the application layer of the OSI model, POP3 is an Internet protocol used for delivering or receiving e-mails.

Postfix
Postfix is a free mail system that works on UNIX systems for the delivery and retrieval of e-mails.

Pretty Good Privacy (PGP)
PGP is a public key encryption system used for e-mail communications.

Procmail
Procmail is used in the UNIX environment as a mail delivery agent (MDA).

QMail
QMail is a mail component used on UNIX systems.

Routing Information Protocol (RIP/RIP2)
Routing Information Protocol finds a route with the smallest number of hops between the source and destination.

SAP—Account Management (FS-AM)
Account Management system used in banking for the administration of customer accounts; provides receivables and payables information between a bank and third parties.

SAP—Accounts Payables (AP)
The Accounts Payable application, a major part of the purchasing system, is a component that records and administers accounting data for vendors, creates journal entries, updates inventory, and automatically makes postings in response to transactions.

SAP—Accounts Receivable (AR)
Part of the sales management system, the Accounts Receivable application records and administers accounting data of all customers.

SAP—Asset Accounting (FI-AA)
The Asset Accounting (FI-AA) component is used for managing and supervising fixed assets within the SAP System.

SAP—Contract Accounts (FI-CA)
Part of SAP ERP Financial Accounting, Contract Accounts is a standard accounts receivable and accounts payable function for managing business partners.

SAP—Controlling (CO)

Controlling provides users with information for management decision making. It facilitates coordination, monitoring, and optimization of all processes in an organization.

SAP—Controlling Profitability Analysis (CO-PA)

Profitability Analysis analyzes the profit or loss of an organization. The system allocates the corresponding costs to the revenues for each segment.

SAP—Cost Center Accounting (CO-OM-CCA)

Cost Center Accounting is used for assigning overhead costs to the business unit in which they occurred.

SAP—Profit Center Accounting (EC-PCA)

Enterprise Controlling (EC) Profit Center Accounting evaluates the profit or loss of independent areas within an organization.

SAP Enterprise Controlling Consolidation (EC-CS)

Enterprise Controlling (EC) Consolidation is an application component that consolidates functions used for external rendering of accounts and internal reporting.

SAP Environment, Health and Safety (EHS)

This SAP component supports users with activities that help manage all areas of industrial safety, health, and environmental protection.

SAP ERP Central Component (ECC)

A replacement for R/3 Enterprise, ECC is structured as the foundational product from which other products are built and developed.

SAP Financial/Management Accounting and Controlling (FI/CO)

Controlling (CO) and Financial Accounting (FI) are independent components in the SAP system, but they both have data flowing between the two components on a regular basis, causing them to be inherently integrated.

SAP Funds Management (FM)

FM is a component in which the funds are managed.

SAP General Ledger (GL)

GL is a structure that records changes to the account during a posting period.

SAP Material Requirements Planning (MRP)
The MRP is used for planning the availability of material, for procuring required quantities for sales and distribution.

SAP Materials Management (MM)
Materials Management is used for ensuring materials are available for production when needed, and also used to monitor the availability of materials.

SAP NetWeaver
SAP NetWeaver provides the application platform that facilitates the implementation of the Enterprise Services Architecture.

SAP Product Cost Controlling (CO-PC)
Product Cost Controlling calculates the costs that occur during manufacture of a product or provision of a service. It enables you to calculate the minimum price at which a product can be profitably marketed.

SAP Sales & Distribution (SD)
Part of the Logistics module, Sales and Distributions deals with sales processes starting from customer quote, sales, orders, invoicing, and billing. Other features included in the SD process are pricing, credit management, tax determination, and availability check.

SAP Supply Chain Management (SCM)
Powered by SAP NetWeaver, SCM is an end-to-end automated and integrated process for SAP users to manage and collaborate with partners, vendors, and customers in their supply network.

SAP Transportation Management System (TMS)
A graphical tool used to organize, perform, and monitor transports (work flows, requests, etc.) between SAP Systems.

SAP Warehouse Management Systems (WMS)
This functionality manages the internal movement and storage of materials in a warehouse system.

Secure Shell (SSH)
SSH is a network protocol used for authenticating communications when logging onto a remote computer.

Sendmail
Similar to Postfix, Sendmail is a message transfer agent (MTA) used for the delivery and retrieval of e-mails.

Simple Mail Transfer Protocol (SMTP)
Simple Mail Transfer Protocol is a TCP/IP protocol used in the process of sending and receiving e-mails.

Simple Network Management Protocol (SNMP)
Simple Network Management Protocol allows network administrators to connect to and manage network devices.

Source Code Control (CVS, RCS, SCCS)
CVS—Concurrent Version System—is a free source control application that developers use to manage the versioning of their code. Same as RCS—Revision Control System and SCCS—Source Code Control System.

Switched Multimegabit Data Service (SMDS)
Switched Multimegabit Data Service is a WAN with speeds of 1.544 to 45Mbps.

Synchronous Optical Network (SONET)
Synchronous Optical Network identifies how fiber-optic technology can deliver voice, data, and video over network speeds over 1Gbps.

Telnet
Telnet is an Internet protocol that allows users to connect their PCs as remote workstations to a host computer anywhere in the world and use that computer as if it were local. Telnet allows terminal emulation, which is the ability to access a remote computer and use its resources.

Transmission Control Protocol/Internet Protocol (TCP/IP)
Transmission Control Protocol/Internet Protocol is used in the interconnection of computers on the Internet.

User Acceptance Test (UAT)
AKA end-user testing, this is the type of testing performed by customers on a production system to approve, accept, and sign off on a project.

User Datagram Protocol (UDP)
User Datagram Protocol provides a connectionless transportation service on top of the Internet Protocol (IP).

Virtual Private Network (VPN)
The extension of a private network, including encapsulated, encrypted, and authenticated links across shared or public networks.

Wide Area Network (WAN)

A Wide Area Network is a data communications network that is geographically separated. WAN computer networks usually span several locations.

X Windows System

X Windows is a software program used in the UNIX environment that provides a graphical user interface (GUI) much like a Windows system.

Index